C000297727

THE FLOOD

Surviving the Deluge

MICHAEL BROWN

Michael Brown

Merlin Unwin Books

CONTENTS

To all our grandchildren

ACKNOWLEDGEMENTS

First and foremost we'd like to give huge and lasting thanks to our family for all their support through the flood days: especially to my brother, Alastair, and his wife, Kathy, for looking after Poppy for nearly three months; to my sister, Diana, and to Emily and Oliver who were in contact daily to see how we were faring, as well as to all the cousins and friends in distant places who made frequent contact to boost our spirits.

In works of non-fiction it is common for authors to thank those who have helped in their research or lent special insights into the writing of their book. Whilst warmly thanked for their contribution they often do not actually appear within its pages. In theatrical terms, they remain behind the scenes.

This book is different. As the events of the flood are based on the diary I kept during that time, many of those who gave such kindness and support to Utta and myself throughout those watery days actually figure as part of the narrative – 'Tonight went to supper with..' Furthermore it was these encounters, perhaps sitting round a table having a meal or a cuppa with them that often led to conversations and stories of their lives or the lives of others which also form part of this book.

And so it is with extra special gratitude that we would like to thank all those who helped us in so many different ways during the flood, either taking in our washing or inviting us round for meals or lending us essential items we'd lost or giving us food to take home, or helping restore order, or simply popping by to share a coffee and a chat. And for telling their stories. For all or some of these things and much more, we are hugely grateful to Roddy and Holly Baillie-Grohman, Rita and Chris Dobson, Nick and Sheila Frost, Sue and Glen Ward, Harry and Chris Osmond, Simon and Jayne Taylor,

Rose Burton, Evie Body, John and Becky Coutts, Niall Christie, Tony Roberts, Michael and Judith Drewell, Liz and Peter Nightingale, David and Ingrid White, Biddy and Paul Belding, Sam and Lucy Hay, John and Margaret Spurr, Tony and Susan Ogilvy, Jane Lang, Nigel Hunt, Nigel and Kate Bunce, Carolyn Roche, Miriam Arscott, Julian and Diana Temperley.

I'd also like to thank all those who gave me their time – and their coffee – to talk about their involvement in the flooding and their memories past and present. They include Richard and Anne England, Alastair and Mary Mullineux, Rob Walrond, James Winslade, Simon Taylor, Mike and Jenny Curtis, Chris Osborne, Nick Frost, Carolyn Roche, Julian and Mary Taylor, Sally England, Graham and Helen Walker, John and Lizzie Leach, Dion Warner, Sally Dunbar, and Michele and Terry Bradley. I am also indebted to two excellent books in particular for the background and history of the Levels: 'Avalon and Sedgemoor' by Desmond Hawkins and 'The Draining of the Somerset Levels' by Michael Williams as well as to Geoffrey Body and Roy Gallop's booklet on the 'Parrett River Trade.'

I'd like to thank James Crowden not only for his supply of pies but for bringing Martin Hesp to witness and write about the Thorney flood and for introducing us, with Pauline Rook, to Dan Alsop, chartered engineer, who saw the potential of the Raised Bank to protect the village. I'd like to give special thanks to Ed Colegrave and his team for renovating and repairing the house after the flood with such spirit and understanding – not often said of builders! I'd also like to thank our neighbour, Nick Frost, as well as all the movers and shakers in Somerset County Council directly involved, for ensuring the Thorney Raised Bank was built and the splendid team from Bernard Perry Ltd who carried out the work.

Chapter 1

IN THE BEGINNING

'What about flooding', we asked nervously when we looked at the crumbling house as prospective buyers all those years ago.

'No, it never floods now,' they said, 'Not after all the work they did back in the 1950s and 1960s raising the bank,' and they were right. Mind you, we'd probably have bought the place anyway, it was love at first sight for Utta.

That was back in 1982. Now we are sitting on that same riverbank with a cup of tea. It is spring, 2012, on the river Parrett at Thorney on the edge of the Somerset Levels.

This is reward time after an afternoon of heavy gardening. The grassy bank is dry now. After weeks of cold wind the weather has changed, the earth in the veg garden beginning to warm to the fingers; this has led to a fever of planting. As we sip our tea we watch the comings and goings of a pair of kingfishers on the bank opposite. They're busy either making a nest in the bank behind them or using their perch of tangled sticks as a fishing platform. There's been much activity up and down the river these last few days. Like jewels they flash past, skimming low over the water down the middle of the river following the sweep of the bend. Elsewhere below us there's a plop, a ruffle of water as the fish are starting to feed. Big chub gather on this stretch; at the moment the water is too dark to see into but in summer they stack like torpedoes in the shallows under the far bank. And spring has sprung: we've just seen the first swallow.

Though teeming with wildlife there is nothing spectacular about this river which winds idly past between its high banks. You could easily pass it by, just another unremarkable stretch of the river Parrett. In the big field opposite along the far hedge a heron stalks the long grass like an old man looking for his glasses. Peering intently. Frogs, mice, insects, we never know, but he's often there. Beyond the hedge is the old railway line that linked Yeovil to Langport running past the old milk depot, ugly red brick buildings to our left. From here the milk churns were loaded onto the stopping trains and straight up to London to the Nestlé factory – always known locally as 'nestles', they didn't bother with that new-fangled accent on the last 'e'. Later the buildings were taken over by the Milk Marketing Board serving the many small dairy farmers round here. As if in memory a rusty old churn we found by the railway line now forms the centrepiece of our veg patch. The depot buildings are used today by small businesses, a forge, carpenter, stone mason. Noises of banging, metal bashing punctuate the peace each day.

Not the scene on the manicured banks of the river Avon or the Test, no, just a very ordinary corner of the Somerset Levels. But we love it, love this spot, our house and our garden sheltered by hedge and trees and the big house across the road. We called it Willow Cottage when we bought it as a ruin thirty years ago but it appears on old maps of the early 1900s as the Withy Factory and belonged to local agricultural merchants, processing the withies – willows – grown on the moor behind us for the basket-making trade. From our seat on the bank, the house stands behind and below us, settled into the curve of the river in such a way that it seems almost to grow out of the ground it stands on. The larger part, perhaps once the manager's house, is built of the local blue lias stone, weathered now, while the oldest, smaller part is of rose-coloured brick, thin and irregular, like home-baked biscuits, hauled up over two centuries ago by barge from the thriving brickworks at Bridgwater on the mouth of the Parrett. The barge might well have carried coal and other products and returned with a load of withies or flour from the mill upstream. Processing withies was evidently thirsty work and required a sizeable workforce for when we first discovered the house in its ruined state there were urinals everywhere, inside and out, though this might also have had something to do with the presence of the pub next door, 'The Old Rising Sun'.

Behind us, over the road, is West Moor, one of a patchwork of moors, tracts of low-lying land, each with their own individual character with names like King's Moor, Currymoor, Saltmoor, Allermoor, which together form the Somerset Levels. Some are as big as prairies but 'our' West Moor, around 800 acres, is one of the smallest, and most contained; in the eyes of all those who live around its edge it's by far the most beautiful, bounded by the river Parrett and the river Isle and the villages and hamlets of Kingsbury, Lower and Higher Burrow and Hambridge to the south. Like all the moors on the Levels it is criss-crossed by a maze of rhynes – water ditches – enclosing the fields. On average one square mile contains as many as twenty miles of rhyne. Low-lying, much of it is at sea level or just above.

One of the things that attracted us to Willow Cottage when we first stumbled across it back in the early 1980s was the fact that you could simply cross the road and walk for miles on droves, green lanes, that take you deep into the moor alongside rhynes fringed with reeds busy in summer with the flicker and sound of warblers that you can only ever glimpse. Like all the moors it has a tranquillity, a deep peace and intimacy that holds you, causes you to stop and stare, to dream. It teems with wildlife: otters leave trails of fresh water mussels; warblers; skylarks in spring; snipe and lapwing reside in winter. Swans make huge nests in the same place each year. There are redshank, cranes, egret, water voles, butterflies; dragonfly as big as choppers take off and land on lily pads in summer. And always a heron like a sentinel peering into the rhyne or river. The moor is a great rich soup supporting growth of all forms of life, willow, grass, cattle and wildlife.

Not so long ago our local West Moor was covered in withies, the basket-making variety of willow, the wands planted seventy thousand to the acre. Many families around the edge of the moor had a withy bed or two down on the moor. It was probably the largest industry in the area employing hundreds of people and entire families. Houses would often have their own withy boilers where the bundles of wands were boiled to soften the bark for stripping. Some still exist on the road to Kingsbury, the next village; with their brick chimneys and chambers they're like old-fashioned steam engines stripped of their wheels. Children would do an hour's work, stripping the bark by hand before and after school.

When we first came here many of the withy beds were still worked. I remember one evening following a grassy lane between tall sedges that swayed and rustled in the gloom, beyond them an impenetrable mass of withies. It was like entering some strange jungle, so unexpected, a totally different world. The withies were harvested over winter, cut, often boated up to the edge of the village in the floodwater for processing at farms and houses along the moor, many of them at our house, the Withy Factory, here in Thorney. Now, the market gone, just two withy beds remain. West Moor has changed, more sparse. But still magical.

In time of flood it acts as a massive sump to park the floodwater from the rivers and surrounding hills, storing it sometimes for months at a time before it can be pumped back into the river Parrett.

Most years there is flooding of some sort and the moor fills for a week or two; there is something ancient, elemental about this inland winter sea on our door step that brings great flocks of wildfowl, widgeon, teal, geese and swan. We have seen some huge floods, roughly one a decade, that have threatened inundation but mostly it's been a case of the odd road impassable, soggy gardens and the inconvenience of having to go the long way round to get to where you want. Seasonal flooding of the moor has become part of our life as it was for those who lived on and around the Levels down the centuries.

And so for three decades we have stayed dry. As they said we would.

*****

Neither of us are locals. Utta is Australian, her family having emigrated there from Germany when she was seven, while I spent my early childhood in north Cornwall before my parents moved to the edge of Dartmoor in Devon. Those were the only moors I knew, high moors, where we spent most of our summers roaming and swimming in freezing moorland streams. Travelling home to Devon down the A30 or A303 from school or university or from work in London I always found Somerset featureless and uninspiring; glimpses of elms, dull fields, flat landscape, my mind always focussed on getting home to Devon and Dartmoor.

And then in the spring of 1973 quite by chance I discovered the Somerset Levels.

I was asked by a friend if I'd like to help catch elvers – baby eels – which he was shipping to eel farms in the Far East for growing on. I'd left a job in industry and was at the time trying to earn my living as a free-lance travel writer. With limited success. I'd spend hours staring at blank pieces of paper or crossing out the few lines I'd written. The invitation to Somerset was a delicious diversion. The first night of my visit I was dropped with a net and some brief instructions on how to catch them on the bank of the river Parrett about two miles below Langport opposite a small pub, the Black Smock, whose lights shone softly over the river. To my surprise I caught a few kilos, tiny wriggling creatures, translucent, unmistakable baby eels that made a faint whispering in the back of the net when I lifted it to inspect my catch.

It was all exciting, all new. I'd never stood on a river bank at night, I'd never fished for elvers, I'd never seen the Somerset Levels, nor even heard of them before. It was a mild soft spring night and gradually as I fished I began to tune in to the sounds, the mew of peewits, cough of cattle in the field opposite, a church clock striking somewhere and an owl on the hill behind. I was hooked.

When you grow up in a place as a child you may love it, feel happy there, but you've had no part in choosing that place. Then comes a time when you meet a new and different landscape, one that totally grabs you, one that you make your own. This was Somerset for me. As the days went by, in gaps between fishing tides, I became enchanted by the wide open skies, the quiet lanes lined with willows, and always the glint of water from rhyne or river. And out there on the moor, that deep settled peace.

Yet it wasn't only Somerset that drew me, so different to anything I'd seen before, it was the prospect of finding a new direction, a new way of life. I'd found it hugely satisfying helping with the elvers, making nets and all the hands-on practical stuff as well as finding markets for them. The following year when I returned to help again, things had moved on, the Far East market for elvers had evaporated and my friend had been offered a place at a business school. He suggested I might like to take on the elver business. I leapt at the idea. Being my own boss, running a small business, and in the country. It solved the problem of how and where to earn a living. There was nothing to buy, just the lease to renegotiate with the farmer.

By the start of the elver season of spring 1975 I'd found a cottage at a peppercorn rent on the Blackdown Hills within easy reach of the elver-holding site and the river. Much more important I'd found someone to share this new rural life. That Christmas I'd sent a card to a striking and unusual Aussie lady I'd met in London; she'd been over in Europe for a year or two having a break from nursing but was now back in Sydney. I told her about the elvers and the cottage and for fun described the little bath, the smallest I'd ever seen that sat in the windy lean-to tacked on to the side of the cottage. Posting the card I'd thought no more of it. Then one day, some three weeks later, a man on a motorcycle delivered a telegram – as they did in those days (far more romantic than a text or an email). It read quite simply, 'Coming to share your bath'.

And she did.

That first elver season of 1975 we had beginners' luck: a plentiful supply of elvers, good fishermen – we caught most of them ourselves – and a good market for them for restocking in Germany. We made a small profit. It was exhilarating. We were married in the September. The following year our beginner's luck ran out. The elver season was very thin and we just survived. Utta went back to nursing and I found some part-time teaching but we carried on the elvering and good years were to follow. We'd learned a lesson though: man could not live by elvers alone. They were too unreliable. There needed to be something more secure. Gradually and more by drift and happenstance than by bold decision, we began to develop a smokery, producing smoked eel and in time all sorts of other smoked food. We sold by mail order, then through our on-site shop and finally opened a restaurant in the building next door.

In the long hot summer of 1976 we'd moved from the Blackdown Hills to a rented house in Drayton, home for six years, but we were always looking for a place of our own. The trouble was we had no identifiable income with which to reassure the mortgage companies; we were self-employed with an erratic business, they'd take one look at our accounts and politely show us the door. Then Utta found Willow Cottage. She was on her way back from work and saw the derelict building with a *For Sale* sign. It had a demolition order on it, geese lived in one end, floors and ceilings were collapsing. But it was south facing, it flooded with sunlight – very important for an Aussie – and she could see the potential. I was not ecstatic. All I could see were the costs of renovation. But there had been two significant changes, the banks had entered the mortgage market and were touting for customers, and the council was handing out house improvement grants.

We bought it. The builder knocked most of it down and rebuilt it in accordance with modern regulations which gave us higher ceilings and yet more light. Thoughtfully too, as he'd had experience of flooded properties, he raised the old floor level by about six inches.

We moved into our new house in early summer of 1983. And for the rest of our working lives, through all the years of elvering, Utta's nursing, the growing up of our children, developing the smokery through to retirement and the arrival of grandchildren, all through a full and busy life, Willow Cottage was our home, our harbour. A place we loved. Root down deep.

And in all that time it never flooded.

*****

When you arrive in a new place you often learn about it by degrees like getting to know a person. When first coming to Somerset I was totally unaware of the history of flooding on the Levels. Probably it was through chatting to Ernie Woods, the shepherd, at the farm where we had the elver storage tanks that I had my first insight into what the flooding had been like in the old days. As I worked in the barn making nets or trays each season, he liked to come in and chat after he'd done his rounds of the sheep – he was a great talker. But he was fascinating, a rich seam of oral history. Ernie had lived down on the moor in a cottage on the river, a two-up-two down, about two miles below Langport. I remember him describing some of the big floods he'd seen as a boy in the 1930s.

'We'd take what we could carry upstairs and I kin remember one time it were so deep, we ad to get in and out the house through the bedroom window. We had an old boat and 'ad her tied up to the winda sill. Then when the water was gone out the house we just gave it a good brushing out to get rid of that there mud and stuff and then we got on wi' it. There waddn no insurance or nothun in them days. No, you just got on wi en.'

Another person with memories of the flooding is Dion Warner, a retired engineer, a great naturalist and now regular volunteer for the RSPB and Natural England. As a child he was evacuated from London during the war and joined his grandparents who lived on the river Parrett at Stathe, up-river from the confluence of the Tone and the Parrett. His grandfather was a ditcher, working for the Drainage Board, paid by the chain, 22 yards of ditch cleared.

'There was always flooding every winter. You just got used it, a bit of water came in the house, no one minded too much, you just brushed it out. But they really worked the sluices then. That was the way you managed the river: you waited till low tide and then you wound up the hatches on the sluice gates and let the flood water out of the moor. So every stretch of the river had its sluice and person responsible for operating it.' He has other memories too, of his grandfather catching eels. 'He used to set night lines, baited with chicken gizzards. I can remember him coming home with an eel over the handle bars of the bike trailing over the road. Big ones like that, they'd bake, stuffed with parsley sauce.' Back then you lived on the moor and you lived off the moor.

Whenever Dion was taken by his grandfather – it was always a Sunday – to have his hair cut by Harold Mead, a withy grower and cider maker in Athelney, grandpa would sit outside in the garden shed sampling the cider. Dion meanwhile was given his short back and sides in a room where one wall was scored with the heights and dates recording all the floods that had entered the house over the years. And there were many.

Flooding wasn't all bad though and it could bring unexpected benefits. One particularly bad winter probably in the late 1920s a couple were living upstairs in their flooded house. From the landing, the story goes, the husband spotted a large fish swimming around below them in the parlour,

'I said to the missus, we're going to ave 'ee. So I went and got me gun and I shot the bugger. Eee were a gurt big carp and we 'et en. Twas lovely.' It was quite possibly in the same flood that a farmer milked his cows on a bridge, the only dry spot on his land, while his wife continued to churn butter on the roof of one of their outbuildings.

Hearing these stories and reminiscences, one is struck by the resilience, the toughness of people 'back in them days,' how long-suffering they were. It may have helped that their working lives were hard with few material possessions beyond the basics, with stone flag floors rather than carpets – the more you have, the more you fret – yet one senses, beside the sense of community, a greater self-reliance, more communal responsibility in coping with the flood. Living on the moor men knew the river far more intimately than we do now; they worked on it and on its rhynes; they knew how and where you might control the flood, to wind sluices, and they were permitted, indeed expected, to do so. It was much more hands-on then. There is no way that we would know how to start the pumps at our nearby pumping station – even if we could get into the building. It'd be a criminal offence, rightly so. Over time management of the river and flooding has been centralised, with fewer and fewer boots on the ground and with that, something has been lost; such a remotely managed system can lead to suspicion, anger, to frustrated cries of 'Why aren't they doing anything?', 'Why aren't they pumping?' Good management is also about good communication.

*****

Gradually I came to realise that you had only to dip into any history of the Somerset Levels or talk to older members of the community and it was always there: the threat of flooding from the river or the sea. As relevant today as it was a thousand years ago.

And if you glance at the map of the county, you can see why: the Somerset Levels are a flood waiting to happen. For a start, bounded on all sides by hills, like shuttering, the Mendips in the east, the Quantocks to the west, the Blackdowns and the Ham hills to the south, the whole upland area that drains onto the Levels is some four times greater an area than the Levels themselves: four into one doesn't go. Added to this, the plain of the Levels is actually saucer-shaped, turning up along the coastal ridge, marginally higher than the moors inland, preventing the rapid escape of waters.

When rain falls on the hills it feeds rapidly – increasingly so with urban expansion upstream – in to these rivers which are amongst some of the slowest-moving in the country. The Parrett has a fall of about one foot for every mile on its way down to Bridgwater. Like an old dairy cow, it moves slowly, not to be rushed, taking its time to make it to the parlour, always with an eye for the chance of a wander where it shouldn't. So instead of rushing their cargo of water to discharge into the sea like any other well-behaved river, there's something truculent, bloody-minded about these rivers of the Levels. Despite centuries of efforts at banking them up, fastening them in, they have a tendency to unbutton, go walk about, outwards, sideways – in often devastating fashion.

And if all that wasn't enough – this saucer-shaped plain, bounded by hills, drained by the lazy rivers – there is the tidal lock: even if they wanted to discharge into the sea, the second largest tidal system in the world roars up the Bristol Channel and blocks the Parrett at periods of high tide – six days out of every fortnight – for about three hours twice a day. Like having a huge barrier set in place at the river outlet. No wonder then that down the centuries to the present day it has been a constant struggle to keep the sea out and the river in.

*****

Thousands of years ago it must have been an extraordinary landscape, this wilderness of swamp and marsh, an inland sea swaying and swishing with great beds of reed stretching as far as the eye could see, dotted with small islands covered in thickets of alder and willow; the air full of the cries of birds, the waters teeming with fish. A good place for its early dwellers settled around the edges or on some of the larger islands, moving by boat, canoe, or on a network of wooden trackways, like the Sweet Track, constructed around 3800BC, laid across the marsh like spines.

From Neolithic times man had realised the value of those parts of the marshy wastes that weren't permanently submerged, as grazing lands for fattening their cattle. Somerset was originally known as 'Sumersata', the land of the summer people who came down from the hills to graze their animals. Flood silt like the Nile in ancient Egypt enriched the land and the grass grew.

For the hunter gatherer, for communities living off the Levels, there was no need to change the landscape, it provided all they needed. The Levels could stay as they were. But for farmers, early graziers, it was different: they realised that where land was not submerged all year round, when it became uncovered in summer and on the islands, the grass grew on soil enriched by silt and nutrients and gave good pasture for their animals. Proper agriculture required better drainage to increase the acreage available and to improve the conditions for people to live on and around the moors.

It's easy to think it might have been the Romans who began to sort out the drainage and flooding of the Levels. They were such incredible engineers and after all, if they could build Hadrian's Wall 120 miles long in just six years across the north of the country to keep the barbarians out, they could surely manage a few miles of sea wall along with some draining of the marshes. But it seems they were never much interested in the Levels. It wasn't strategically or economically important enough for them. Yes, they mined silver and lead on the Mendips, and they were indeed involved in some major engineering, building sea defences; they also found the best places ways to ford the Parrett – at Combwich on the estuary and up-river inland at Langport – but they liked to be able to move fast, none of this sloshing about in a swamp if you could avoid it. So they seemed happier on higher ground, flood-free, building their settlements, like Ilchester, more in south Somerset nearer to their military road, the Fosse Way that sliced across the country linking Exeter to Lincoln, a distance of 182 miles and never more than six miles from a straight line.

In the early Middle Ages the Anglo-Saxons with their settlements and intensification of farming on and around the islands of the Levels – recognisable today through the suffix of oy, ney, and y as in Muchelney, Middlzoy and Othery – would almost certainly have made some attempts at improving the land. At this time, however, the wetlands of Somerset were used in other ways. In time of war they were a perfect hiding place; no enemy would dare follow you into this labyrinth of reed and marsh. In 871 when the whole region was invaded by the Danes, Alfred, Anglo-Saxon King of Wessex, took refuge from their forces, retreating into this watery jungle to his base on the island of Athelney, the perfect hide-out from which to re-group.

Legend has it that during this interlude, in hiding on the island of Athelney, he was asked to keep an eye on bread or cakes baking in the oven of his host's house. One can imagine the scene: Alfred and his commanders, heads bent over a map at a rough table, absorbed in planning their next move. One of them, suddenly, 'My Lord, what's that smell, something burning?'

Alfred, raising his head, sniffing, puzzled, then suddenly, 'Oh bugger it, (or the Saxon equivalent) the cakes, quick, I forgot the cakes...'

We can all sympathise with the poor man, he wasn't the first and he certainly won't be the last. He was obviously better at fighting than he was at cooking for in May 878 he emerged from the marshes, surprising the Danes and defeating them in battle. Under the terms of surrender Guthrun, their leader, agreed to convert to Christianity. As a result the Danish King and his chiefs were baptised at Aller, across the moor from Athelney.

*****

Managing the seasonal flooding of the Levels that occurred down the centuries needed constant attention, commitment and funds. It also required continuity of purpose and the constant need for maintenance. That is as true now as it was in the Middle Ages. From the end of the first millennium to the present day, the draining of the Levels has been characterised by periods of sustained progress followed by long fallow periods of muddle and inactivity.

It was the church that had perhaps the greatest effect on the landscape of the Levels. The Benedictine monasteries of Glastonbury, Muchelney and Athelney, together with the great See of Bath and Wells, all with their ecclesiastical estates, were major landowners and provided the commitment and funds in reclaiming and draining the Levels. Their main achievements took place in the thirteenth and fourteenth centuries but nevertheless for several hundred years until their dissolution in the 1530s they were the consistent administration. They had the wealth, energy and purpose to mobilise the workforce needed to embank rivers, dig rhynes and ditches, build miles of retaining walls – even to alter the course of rivers. All serious undertakings. Indeed it was in their own interests. Through ingenious cuttings and use of rivers, Glastonbury and Wells both had direct access to the sea and trade, while draining the Levels not only improved the land but created more acreage for grazing. Upgrading mere pasture to meadows meant that hay crops could be grown for over-wintering animals, improving the settlements and yielding better rentals from tenants: in 1234, for example, the accounts of Glastonbury abbey record 722 acres of reclaimed land near Weston Zoyland, increased to 972 acres by 1240 and all producing more revenue for the coffers.

However the momentum of these achievements was lost by the ravages of the Black Death in 1348 when nearly half the population was wiped out, further by the strife and chaos of the Wars of the Roses and finally by the dissolution of the monasteries themselves in the 1530s. Throughout this time, of course, the problems remained: seasonal flooding could still turn the whole area into a watery waste. Yet without the sustained commitment of the church, the progress that had been made gradually unravelled; land ownership fragmented and on such a disparate group of tenants and landowners it became increasingly difficult to raise taxes to fund works needed.

For the ensuing centuries, indeed right up until the Second World War, progress on the draining and improvement of the Levels remained sporadic: years of intense activity followed by barren years of muddle and decline. Great opportunities were lost. In 1655 the great Dutch engineer, Cornelius Vermuyden, who had famously drained the Fens, purchased 4000 acres of 'boggy and unwholesome' land on the Kings Sedgemoor that he aimed to improve by drainage; if successful he would almost certainly have been asked to drain the rest of the moor. However the scheme was rejected by the commoners, tenants and freeholders who refused to give their consent fearing for the loss of their grazing rights and their livelihood.

Again it is hardly surprising that after the Civil War, followed by Monmouth's Rebellion and its savage reprisals, matters of drainage and reclamation were far from the minds of men. As a result, two thirds of the Levels were still un-reclaimed nearly a century later. It wasn't until around the 1770s, however, that things began to change. Growth in agriculture brought renewed activity in the draining of the Levels: expanding markets, a growing population, importance of food supply during the Napoleonic Wars and a rise in land values (an acre of land valued at £20 could be worth up to a £100 if drained), provided all the right economic conditions to reawaken a sense of purpose. The Enclosure Acts enabled land on the moor to be enclosed often by the creation of rhynes, water boundaries, along with channels and ditches which also helped improve drainage. Steam pumps began to be used for the first time not just to prevent flooding but also to extend the period of the grazing season further into the spring and autumn. Pumping stations were built up and down the river and at crucial points on the moor. Many are still in use today – though electric has replaced first steam then diesel power. Their tall brick chimneys still mark the landscape up and down the river.

The Westonzoyland Pumping Station is a good example. It was built following the 1830 Act of Parliament to drain and improve the moors around Othery, Middlezoy and Westonzoyland. It drained 2000 acres of surrounding land. The first pump, not powerful enough, was replaced by a unique Land Drainage pump, made in 1861 by Easton Amos, a masterpiece of Victorian engineering, capable of pumping a 100 tonnes a minute, a match for most modern equipment. The pumping station is now a museum – open every Sunday – and offers a fascinating insight into a way of life that lasted pretty well from the mid-1830s through to the 1950s. A remote spot, the station keeper lived on site with his wife and family in the little cottage provided by the Water Board built next to the pump. Far from help in time of flood, they had to be entirely self-sufficient. They had their own vegetable garden, their own forge to make any running repairs to the pump or steam engine – and of course their own outside lavatory – that leans at an alarming angle. Very probably they used the fire box in the boiler stove for their baking and roasting, as do the volunteers who run the place now.

Back in the early days of elvering in the 1970s I remember these pumps being turned on as the river swelled on the high tide each spring. They were diesel-driven then but made a wonderful clonk-clonk-clonk sound in the gathering dusk. It let you know that somewhere out there a sweet flow of fresh water from the moor was being pumped into the river to lure the elvers into the side. It drew them like a drug. In festive atmosphere family and friends of the pump keeper would gather for the occasion as they would have done down the years long before elvering became commercial. Elvers were prized seasonal food, a little luxury after a long winter, and the ducks loved them too. One night I remember fishing opposite one of these pumps just below Burrowbridge. On my side of the river I was catching almost nothing while I watched, wild with envy, netfulls of elvers being scooped out on the opposite bank.

I'd always imagined the Victorians with their engineering skills would have made great advances in draining and improving the Levels. But they didn't. There was small progress but it was sporadic, scattered and often only maintained the status quo. Rivalries between vested interests frequently crippled any real progress. Projects and schemes abounded but were turned down or failed to materialise for lack of funds. A plan to improve the outfall of the lower Parrett, for example, in the late 1800s was firmly rejected by the owners of the slime batches – the works that produced the famous Bath Brick, a popular cleaning stone – situated along the banks in that part of the river. What was lacking was a coherent, integrated plan for the Levels. And so as projects and schemes came and went, so too did the winter flooding.

When exploring the moors slowly on foot or by bike, you become aware that they are a great patchwork, a spider's web of works and installations old and new. They are a landscape bearing the imprint, layer on layer, of the centuries of effort to drain and manage them. What's remarkable is that many of the older structures still operate and play their part in flood defence today. It reminds one of the insides of a great, intricate clock, ancient and rickety, that still works, mostly, but needs constant maintenance.

*****

Down the centuries the sea and the floods have come and gone, part of life, of living on the Levels, yet now and then over the years some have been so huge, so savage, as to be etched in the memory. It's easy to forget that these days flooding is caused mostly by swollen rivers. In earlier times, however, it could just as well have been the sea. Sea defences in particular were often in dire need of maintenance, weakened by years of subsidence. Large parts of the Somerset plain are already below sea level; during big spring tides the sea could be fifteen or twenty feet higher. A breach in a sea wall could allow the tide to pour through miles inland. Terrible enough to be flooded by the river bursting its banks, it must have been utterly terrifying when the sea broke through the defences.

Just such a disaster happened on January 20th 1607 when the tide piled high by gale force winds tore up the Bristol Channel. A tidal wave of sea water breached the sea walls and rushed in for miles over the moor, flooding a huge area, catching people by surprise and causing devastation and loss of life. Some thirty villages were submerged, houses swept away, Glastonbury surrounded by sea water. In the whole Bristol Channel area two thousand or more people perished in the disaster. Though seen at the time as God's warning to the people of England, it seems likely that the event was caused by a storm surge, a combination of high tide and wind driving the vast mass of sea water into the narrowing arms of the Channel so that it literally piled up and overtopped all defences.

In about 2004, however, fresh research came up with a new theory. Records at the time of the 1607 disaster mentioned the sea seeming to recede before coming in at incredible speed catching watchers unawares. As it advanced it seemed to throw off a fog of strange light, like sparks off the top of the wave. These contemporary descriptions, it was suggested, support the supposition that this might well have a tsunami caused by some geological collapse or shift in the ocean floor west of Ireland. Whatever the cause, it must have been terrifying.

In the porch of the peaceful little church at Kingston Seymour close to the coast, just south of Clevedon on the Bristol Channel, and scene of some of the greatest damage, a small wooden board records that 'many Persons were drowned and much Cattle and Goods were lost; the water in the church was five feet high.' It is signed 'William Bower'. This simple plaque with its quiet voice from long ago speaks directly to us and somehow brings much closer the loss of life in that disaster.

Parts of the village were again flooded again in very similar circumstances in December 1981 when a combination of wind and tide caused a surge in sea levels adding four and a half feet to a 24-foot high tide. It overwhelmed seven miles of sea defences in the Bridgwater area, flooding 12,500 acres of land with great loss of livestock and it also flooded one of the reactors at Hinkley nuclear power station. Alongside the plant was Marine Farm, an enterprise set up in the early 1970s, using the waste heat from the cooling towers, to produce eels grown from elvers – baby eels – that we and others supplied each spring. One of the team working there on that day told me that he was at his desk in the office when he suddenly saw a wall of water bearing down about to engulf them. They just got out in time; the whole site was badly damaged.

This was all part of a particularly savage spell of weather that affected the south west of England. Just six days later on 19th December the Penlee lifeboat from Mousehole set out in hurricane force winds and huge seas in an attempt to rescue a stricken Danish vessel near the Wolf rock off the tip of Cornwall but she foundered and was lost with all eight members of the crew.

After 1607, nothing on this scale happened for nearly a century until the Great Storm of early December 1703 when the whole of southern England was hit by hurricane force winds that came in from the west, (not dissimilar to the Great Storm of 1987.) The damage was huge, some fifteen thousand lives were lost and many ships wrecked around the coast. In Somerset the sea swept in again and flooded miles inland, drowning people and thousands of sheep and cattle. Several ships were left stranded in the meadows around Bridgwater. At Wells Bishop Kilder was killed by falling chimneystacks from the palace roof as he slept. After the event Daniel Defoe produced *The Storm* in July 1704 in which he wrote that 'no

pen could describe nor tongue express it.' Coastal towns looked
as if 'an enemy had sackt them'. He describes the terrific winds
that destroyed hundreds of windmills; in some cases the sails
turned so fast that the friction caused the wooden wheels to
ignite and catch fire. As with the disaster of 1607, it was seen
by the church to represent the anger of God against the sins of
the nation.

Now we just blame the Environment Agency.

So the flooding went on down the years, a regular
occurrence, a seasonal expectation, almost unremarkable,
with only the more memorable events rising above the normal
pattern. One of the worst floods in the early part of the
twentieth century was in 1929 when the river Tone broke its
banks and some ten thousand acres were under water from
November to February, the villages of Athelney, Curload and
Stathe all evacuated. In those days when a village on the Levels
flooded, the warning up and down the road was the cry, 'The
bank's gone, the bank's gone,' as the river – or worse still the
sea – burst through a breach in the retaining wall, flooding
cottages, farms, dwellings, spreading across the moor.

Again, what is remarkable reading accounts of these
events is how long-suffering, how tough and adaptable people
were in those days. If you grew up on the moors you were used
to it, it was part of life.

*****

As human beings it is almost as if we need to log and name
great natural events – The Great Flood, the Great Storm, the
Great Snow – and to stow them in the collective memory
to remind ourselves of the power of nature, perhaps also to
remind ourselves how puny we are when nature brushes us
aside, however much we might think we're in control. These
events act, too, as way-markers in our lives, useful pegs on
which to hitch personal memories and dates. Our daughter,
Emily, was born in February 1978 in the midst of the Great
Snowstorm. They inspire in us also a sense of awe and wonder,

they are the stuff of stories told through time by the tribe round the fire, the family round the table.

Floods have always made good stories. Like the tideline left by the high tide, flood waters very definitely leave their mark. Much more difficult to remember how strong the wind blew in the storm, whereas the height of the flood is left there on the wall, a lasting reminder.

When you start to look, you begin to see the markers everywhere. Last year, cycling in France, on the wall of a farmhouse beside the Loire, I spotted a marker three metres above ground with the inscription, 'Hauteur du Cru, décembre 1962'. The French use the word 'cru' – meaning raw, wild – to describe flood water, not the word 'eau' which is what you might drink or bathe in. Similarly a few years ago, on the banks of the Dordogne river in south west France just west of Souillac we came across a squat stone building raised high on a plinth like a small lighthouse set back some fifty meters from the river. For centuries, the power of the Dordogne in spate was used to float the logs felled from the oak forests upstream downriver to Bergerac to be made into barrels for the wine industry. The building was the house of 'le batelier', the ferryman. Into the stone by the door were chiselled the heights of some of the great floods alongside their dates: 1852, 1940 and 1944. There in the green valley beside the beautiful river ruffled by the breeze there was something spellbinding about these markers: awestruck we tried to visualise the height of the water level across the valley, of what it must have been like to see that huge volume of 'cru' – flood water – boring and swirling down the valley. The marks on the wall were testimony to the power of nature. To the beast unleashed.

Chapter Two

THE GATHERING STORM

Once we'd settled in to Willow Cottage in the summer of 1983 and overcome our nervousness that first winter about the risk of flooding, we began to relax and take stock. When the rain came and the river rose to the height of the bank, when the moor filled and the odd road became impassable, then the garden became wet and soggy, often under an inch or two of water. We'd not had the funds to restore the old red brick part of the house so the water would creep under the old back door as it must have done forever and the flagstone floor would darken and sweat. But we didn't mind, that didn't count, we were only using it as a glorified shed. What mattered was that the main part we'd restored, our new home, some six inches higher, was warm and dry.

We learned not to worry, but we learned other things too about the nature of our seasonal flooding. We learned quickly that after heavy rain, the best indicator, better than a rain gauge, was to look at the river itself. Climbing to the top of the bank in the garden we'd inspect the level, read the runes. Often it was a surprise: after a night of persistent rain there'd be little change, still the same river, unaffected, low down, quietly idling by. Then by late morning it'd be up a foot or two, by afternoon up again as the rainfall from the hills and higher ground reached us. It would often be at least twenty-four hours before our stretch of the Parrett really rose. And then, most disconcerting, was how high it came, to within a foot of the top of our bank but – this was vital – well over the top of the *opposite* bank which meant the water could flood the fields the other side and not our garden and house. From its average mean depth, its resting height, the river could rise twelve to fourteen feet, a good four metres between its steeped banks. Others in the village had their own private markers of the extent or potential danger of a flood, 'If it gets near that gate post over there, I know we're in for a big one' or 'I start to get nervous when it reaches the top of the arch under the bridge'.

There were other things we learned too: the fact that, only in exceptional circumstances as when a bank or sea wall breached, most flooding on the Somerset Levels was gradual, by degrees. Not like the streams in the hills that could tear through a house or a village causing devastation before returning within hours to their orderly course. For us on the Levels there'd be a build-up of days, weeks, of rain on rain, of watching the moors fill, the water levels creeping up to the edge of the roads. It gave you time to prepare defences, to move stuff up out of the reach of the water. That was the bonus, the one good thing about our flooding.

The downside though was that it could hang about for a very long time, for weeks, months even. Long enough to pickle you, body and soul.

It was also soon apparent that stories of flooding, like fishing and all natural disasters, involved exaggeration or at least a certain colouring of facts, 'we had three feet of water in the house', or 'cor, when we went through there last night the water was right up over the bonnet.'

In the early years at Willow Cottage, when we saw our first winter floods on the moor and roads around, the boom of the river from the mill upstream was unnerving. We could hear it at night as we drifted off to sleep. Like the roar of the storm or the sea. It was at times like these that you felt compelled to take action and defend the house. Time to get out the pumps and 'let slip the dogs of war'.

Being in the business of keeping eels and elvers alive in tanks before despatch meant that we were well equipped with pumps, knew where to get more and specialist help if it was needed. Yet using pumps is only effective if there is somewhere to pump *from* and somewhere to pump *to*. Luckily Willow Cottage had both. Around the house there were a number of inspection drains under manhole covers where pumps could usefully operate. A cess pit buried in the centre of the drive like a giant onion that held grey water formed a perfect sump for siting bigger pumps. When it came to getting rid of the water we simply pumped back into the river over the bank or via the drain in the road.

There'd always be moments of panic before I got things sorted. I couldn't find the pump or it would be jammed with rubbish from when it was last used, or the outlet pipes were missing. Then I'd have to call up Gordon Small from Muchelney who serviced our pumps at the elver site. Even when he retired he kept spares and a box of fittings and would always get us out of trouble. It was like calling in the doctor in the old days for a sudden emergency. Eventually the system would be working smoothly, the flood water kept at bay.

A real breakthrough came in the early 1990s when we put in a French Drain. This was the idea of a multi-talented man living in Thorney whom we knew as 'Douggy the Digger'. Doug could turn his hand to anything, he'd managed farms, estates, been a farmer; he was also bricklayer, electrician, metalworker, builder. With his own powerful digger, he specialised mostly in ground works and had laid out our drive and garden for us when we renovated Willow Cottage. If anyone else had suggested a French Drain I would have been deeply suspicious as, despite happy memories of time spent in that country, I could still remember the strong whiff of drains from the bowels of the earth – and the nation –

that would hit you in the streets of a French town or village. It was all part of the charm really. No, Doug explained, a French Drain was nothing like that, had nothing to do with sewage disposal; rather it was a deep gravel trench with a slotted pipe at the bottom that intercepted rain or flood water before it reached your property. As we were in the midst of one of our leaner times with the business, the overdraft stretched, there was basically bugger all money to spend on such things so I asked Doug if he would oversee the project while we actually did the work. So, with the help of Johnathan, a student who worked for us in his summer vacation, we dug a trench, a metre deep, round the whole of the old red brick part of the house. We hacked and spaded our way down through blue clay, encountering as we went feasts of oyster shells, pieces of old clay pipes from generations of smokers and enormous, beautiful blue lias slabs, great biscuits of stone, which formed the platform of foundations on which the old house sat. Every so often Doug would drop by to inspect. He'd look all round peering intently into the trench and then pronounce with a slow smile as we waited expectantly,

'No, you gotta go a bit deeper. Tidn deep enough yet.'

But at last it was done, the trench filled with gravel, the pipework connected into an old dustbin sunk deep and acting as a sump by the back door. From then on one pump was always sited there. For years the system worked perfectly, collecting the floodwater, preventing it from entering the old house, the ideal defence. And so we stayed dry.

*****

In the history of the Levels and its flooding there is nothing new under the sun — or the water. After each major flood a recognisable pattern of response is discernible down the centuries: floods come and go, hands are wrung, projects discussed, schemes are promised but as time ticks on and the sun comes out again, momentum and the promise of funds seep away; it all seems a bad dream, it'll never happen again.

Inertia like an old man in his armchair settles comfortably back to sleep. It takes a really big event, a real shock, to cause change as well as the determination to find the funding to carry it through. And so it was very probably the severe flooding of the Levels in 1960 that led to the construction of the three pumping stations in the Langport area, one at Westover by Langport, one at Pidsbury on the Yeo above Langport and 'our' pump at Midelney on the junction of Isle and Parrett. It probably also led, crucially, to the raising of the river bank that borders our house.

The pumping station at Midelney, 'our' pumping station, is about three quarters of a mile downriver from us in Thorney. A characterless, grey building. Almost Soviet style. Built at the head of the main rhyne that drains West Moor, it looks at first sight a bit like a very public lavatory with lots of glass, flat roofed, grey and very functional. Inside, surrounded by dials, consoles, and flashing lights that give it the feel of a 1960s science movie set, sit the three massive pumps that draw the water from the moor through huge pipes nearly a metre in diameter. Each pipe, painted battleship grey (and now green) projects through the wall of the building and bends like a great rounded knee into the river below. At full bore they can haul out 4.6 cubic metres of water per second or 276 cubic tonnes a minute and soon make a dent in any floodwater that may have lain for weeks on West Moor.

That's if they are allowed to pump. For all their potential might the Midelney pumps can remain frustratingly inactive driving us all to distraction for their inertia. This is because the river in flood in front of the pumps is frequently higher than the water in the moor behind: there is nowhere for the water to go. Furthermore there is a protocol, repeated like a mantra over and over by the authorities, that no pumping can take place upstream of Langport while water is discharging over spillways downstream of the town into the moors of Allermoor and King Sedgemoor, endangering the properties in those areas. In vain we are left to ask, 'Yes, but what about our properties?' And there's never really an answer to that.

Sometimes the flood on West Moor would sit for weeks, even months, long after the rest of the moors had been cleared before they turned on the pumps at Midelney. Conspiracy theories abounded, usually based on the myth that some big farmer down river was growing a special crop – I remember it was often carrots – and was being protected from any possible flooding. Or there'd be a theory that they'd lost the key to the pumping station and so couldn't operate the pumps. Most of these conjectures would be prefaced by, 'Well, I heard.....' or 'Somebody told me, no word of a lie....' And from some of the older members of the community, 'They avn a clue wot theym doing. My father used to have a piece of slate and a bit of string and he managed the ....' All of these theories might have been wildly off the mark but they were a measure of the frustration felt by us all. Of the need to have someone, something, on which to vent that frustration. Someone to kick. When you had 800 acres of flooded moor penned up behind a pumping station armed with three massive pumps each capable of delivering so many cubic metres of water a second, it seemed bonkers that it was sitting idle, twiddling its thumbs, watching and waiting. Why bother building it in the first plac? we wondered.

One of the underlying problems was always the lack of information, lack of discussion. When it came to flooding and matters related, it was like living in a totalitarian state. The reason for the pumps not working was always the same: the river level was too high so there was nowhere to pump, or they couldn't pump for fear of causing flooding further downriver. So, grumbling and grudgingly, we accepted that West Moor was again to be used as a parking lot, a huge storage bay, like all the other flooded moors around until such time as the river could absorb the water.

Yet, in truth as long as the flood remained on West Moor, and Thorney stayed dry, it remained just a grumble, a sense of seasonal unfairness that our moor was very often the last of the 'water parking lots' to be drained. And all because of 'they bliddy carrots down there.'

*****

Aside from the vagaries of pumping and despite the fact the Midelney pumping station itself is no architectural beauty, this spot beside the two rivers is one of the most beautiful on the moors. And we have come to love it. The squat outline of the buildings is shaded and softened by the lime trees planted behind it on the bank of the Isle. Beyond on a small slip of an island with a weir to one side and the old half lock on the other, stands a huge white chestnut. Generations of children used to swing over the water from a rope tied to one of the lower branches. The bank scuffed and worn where their feet had pushed off. The chestnut is our visual marker for the progress of spring: some years the looping buds, still whisped with grasses and signs of recent flood, are forming, tight and sticky, even in February, another year it'll be late March. Yet it's always majestic when it flowers, scattering a snowfall of white petals onto the bank and water below. A friendly tree, attracting birds and children. It must be several hundred years old and behind it on the tiny island once stood the lockkeeper's house, now long gone, a tiny two-up and two-down. I once knew an old man in Drayton, the village you can see across Southmoor, who told me that he had lived in the house as a lad before it was demolished.

In the days of the canals when the lock was in use for the barges coming up-river from Langport to Wesport, it must have been a wonderful place to stop a while and have a yarn, exchange news. Maybe share a swig of cider. The walls and chamber of the lock are built of clean cut stone blocks, perfectly formed and indented to fit the lock gates which are no longer there; such fine craftsmanship, nearly two hundred years old, is in stark contrast to the 1960s pump house nearby.

Approaching the spot from Thorney along the river bank, you are on higher ground, though still only a little over nine metres above sea level. This, though, gives unimpeded views across the moors and it is possible on a good day to spot up to nine, even ten, churches, those wonderful fretted towers of the surrounding villages that stand like beacons over the moors: the churches of Long Sutton, Pitney, Muchelney, Huish, Langport, Drayton, Curry, Hambridge and Kingsbury and on a good day even South Petherton. A good game to play with visitors, but binoculars help.

Going through the gate to the site you cross the old sluices, the gravity outfall to the Westmoor main drain, gates that can be wound up to let the flood out. And from time to time they are still used, saving what must be colossal costs of running the pumps. At this spot we tread quietly in the hope of seeing an otter. Fish tend to congregate in the squared inlet beneath the pumps, good fishing for them. They tend to leave their spraints, their dung full of fish bones and shell, marking their territory on the step of the weir beneath the chestnut tree.

Over the years, sadly, signs of the Nanny state have become increasingly evident at the pumping station: weld mesh fences have appeared, protecting us from climbing over the edge and throwing ourselves in front of the sluice gates or the pumps; the rope from which generations of children swung over the river has been removed, an ugly concrete bridge built to take heavier tracked machines onto the moor, and worst of all a rash of warning notices have appeared, 'No Diving', 'No Swimming' 'No Canoeing,' 'Danger,' 'No Entry', Keep out, Keep Clear, Keep Off – thirty or more splattering this small space. Visual litter.

And yet and yet. On a fine evening, with the whisper of the reeds and grasses, the splash of water over the weir, it is a place of deep peace, a magical spot. We always mean to spend a day there, with a book and binoculars and simply wait and watch and listen. Always mean to camp out there one summer's night beneath the lime trees, perhaps hear the otter whistle. But we haven't done so yet. Perhaps it'd be a good place for ashes to be scattered.

But by then there'll probably be another sign, 'No Scattering…!'

*****

It was nearly ten years after we'd moved into Willow Cottage before we had our first real encounter with a big flood, the biggest we'd ever seen. It was February 1990. Roads in and out of the area flooded, even the ones that had always been our escape route. A journey of a few miles would necessitate a huge round trip. It was during the elver season and one night on my way down to Bridgwater to weigh in the fishermen I was blocked by floodwater on every route I tried. Floodwater at night always seems much worse as there is no sense of perspective, you can't gauge where the road is and it's much more difficult to judge depth. The thought of getting stuck and having to abandon the van with all its valuable kit, tanks, oxygen, weighing scales was too much so I turned round and had a peaceful night off instead. Meanwhile Muchelney was completely cut off. Each morning our children were taken to school by tractor, sitting on bales on the trailer as Alan Board, a local farmer, negotiated the road across the moor which was completely submerged, the route only discernible from the tops of hedges and gateposts. Health and Safety would have had a fit but for our children it was a great adventure – something they still remember and will relate to their children.

Others too would remember it. Several houses came very close to flooding that year. The community of Thorney stretches both sides of the river Parret: our side sits on the edge of West Moor while the northern side, closest to Muchelney, borders Thorney Moor. It's here that John Leach has had his pottery since the 1960s and across the road Richard and Anne England farmed at Thorney West Farm, a lovely old farmhouse built of blue lias and ham stone. They kept fierce geese in a little triangular walled plot in front of the farmhouse.

'The farm used to flood, not in the main part of the house, but in the lower parts, round the edges, so we had to keep wellies in the loo for when that happened,' Richard explains.

He had his own special marker, his flood gauge for assessing the depth of the water. 'I drilled a hole down through the floorboards in what we called the Christmas room, which we hardly ever used. And would then drop this piece of bamboo down through the floor.' He holds it up, 'And there it is, you can see the mark, the water was just one inch below the carpet. And there's the date, 14/2/1990. Valentine's Day. The water came right up the lane and across to Johnny. The canoe floated out of the tool shed. Muchelney was cut off for twelve days.'

'Before that,' Anne remembers, 'the worst flood was back in November 1951 when we couldn't get to school in Muchelney, only by horse and cart.'

At Willow Cottage our own pumps were running flat out but coping. We took Emily to choir practice in Muchelney by boat. On the way back the wind had got up, blowing us sideways into the hedge, it was impossible to row, so with my brother who was staying at the time we simply got out and waded, pushing the boat. It was an adventure, one to remember but it was never threatening. And the house stayed dry.

*****

It is a fact of human nature to accept that if something works satisfactorily under normal conditions, then we feel no need to fix it. This can be a dangerous philosophy where flooding is concerned. Gordon Small who often got us out of trouble with our pumps at Willow Cottage worked for Sparrows of Martock, a company long involved with the world of water, pumps, millwheels, and sluices. He knew a thing or two about the river and had strong views about the water authorities, or 'They' as they were usually called, not doing enough dredging. The importance of this had never occurred to me.

'Well it's obvious really,' he'd say, 'if you have a 2-inch pipe and it's blocked by silt so that it's down to an 1' or even half an inch, you're going to notice a huge difference in what it can deliver. So think of that in terms of the river. Which is becoming more and more choked with silt, debris and bank slippage. It needs maintaining. Cleaning out. And they're not doing it. Just look at your stretch here by the house.' And he was right, even in the time we had been in Thorney we'd noticed how the river had narrowed, banks subsided. And we'd never seen any attempt at dredging.

His views are deeply shared by Chris Osborne, director of Oswall Plant Hire in Langport who worked closely with the water board for many years from the 1960s onwards. Chris, also Chairman of Langport Town Council for many years, now retired, is a powerful forthright character who speaks his mind, a passionate advocate of the need for regular maintenance of the river. He has a dim view of the new era of desk-bound bureaucrats with 'their computers and all that stuff'. He was a hands-on engineer, a leader by example, who could hop into any machine and take over its operation if they were a man down. He talks in punchy phrases using his hands to describe and for dramatic effect. It's obvious he loved his work and is affectionately proud of the machines he owned.

Especially the dragline excavators, often known as 'slews' – but he doesn't like that word – that worked not with a fixed arm but with a detachable bucket attached to wire hawsers that could be slung by the 40 foot boom on the machine, rather like a fisherman casting a fly, twenty, fifty metres up or down river and hauled in, giving it enormous reach. Perfect for dredging. He speaks of them with huge affection almost as if they were his family. Made by the engineering company Ruston Bucyrus, they had big clunky box cabs, as big as a hut and great booms like sections of the Eifel tower that must have inspired generations of Meccano enthusiasts. They weren't sexy, didn't have the controlled bulging body builder look that the modern diggers have, but they were very effective and the firm had several of them, as did the River Board. They were in constant use for regular maintenance.

Osborne is adamant about the right machinery for the job. 'Horses for courses,' he says, 'Just because it looks old, doesn't mean it's no good.' And anyway, 'It's not old, it's the best machine for the job.' These machines had huge reach, far, far more than the modern digger, and because of that reach they didn't have to keep moving to reposition which meant that they had very low impact, a vital advantage when working on peat and soft ground like the Levels. Perhaps their greatest advantage was the size of the bucket they could handle. 'No good having all this power if all's you got is a teaspoon on the end,' he says of the modern excavators. His draglines, being so light, could handle a bucket the size of a small garage, shifting huge amounts of spoil or river mud.

In the old days, says Osborne, 'when the old boys had their brains, and not their bloody computers', there was a policy of selective maintenance which the River Board – the Somerset River Catchment authority – would undertake with its own resources and working with contractors like Osborne if the need arose. A system that worked well. Local men with local understanding, boots on the ground, local knowledge, good machinery, dredging the river, cleaning under the bridges. Until the late 1980s. Then in the wave of government sell-offs, the Thatcher government privatised the water authorities, those parts responsible for providing water and sewage services. For a while the river authorities which were part of the whole were left in limbo. However one grave and unintended consequence of the changes was that this also led to the sell-off of great amounts of machinery hitherto owned by the river board, including all the dragline excavators,

'So that when the board went back to being the National Rivers Authority they had no kit and no funds. That was when the trouble started. It was the NRA which lasted until 1996. And then along come this lot, even worse.'

Osborne is scathing about the Environment Agency. Funded by DEFRA (Department for Environment, Food and Rural Affairs), they represent for him remote management in offices by people who have no real understanding of the situation, no hands-on knowledge of the moors nor the machinery to maintain it. The very opposite of what his working life was all about.

'They didn't understand the big picture. All the workshops are gone, turned into offices. That shift from the practical, the machinery, to the office. That says it all. They hadn't a clue. The Parrett's so narrow you could jump the bugger. I'd ask them, 'when are you lot going to clean the river?' And the reply comes back, 'It's not in our brief to clean or dredge the rivers, our brief is to care for the environment.'' Like one of his machines, Osborne is beginning to rev up,

'When the government minister came down after the floods, I told him, 'Get back the old River Boards, get back the workshops, get rid of the EA. Sack the buggers.'

*****

We are often so bound up with our own weather conditions, so used to being shown the weather map of the UK in isolation that we forget that especially here in the south and south west of England we are very much part of continental weather, especially France. What we get here, they are often experiencing as well. In 2000, at the end of the century, as the clocks ticked down to the millennium and we all wondered if our computers would ever work again, we were hit by a series of storms and heavy rain which produced serious flooding similar in size and intensity to 1990. Muchelney was again cut off, returned to its original island state, all roads under water for about two weeks. On New Year's Eve Utta and I rowed down to the church to see in the New Century but with the wind blowing, progress was slow and erratic, especially as we'd lost a rollock for one of the oars. We were rescued by our good friend David White who met us in his waders and towed us the last part. As we reached the church and the millennium gathering, I made a mental note to put chest waders on the shopping list.

Back home at Willow Cottage we'd had the pump running for days but not without the usual flustered beginning:

I'd forgotten where I'd put the pump, the pipes were buried in the hedge, the connectors lost, and it had been so long since the last time that I couldn't remember how everything fitted together. It was a bit like having to put up an elderly tent very quickly in the face of an approaching storm. It was always the same. I never seemed to learn despite my best intentions. Perhaps there was an element of nonchalance creeping in. 'Done this before, it'll be all right'. The garden might become waterlogged, but the bank was as firm and reassuring as ever and any water that collected by the back of the house was collected into the French Drain, then pumped into the river. Anxious friends and family phoned to make sure we were safe and we'd assure them we were well, safe and dry. No cause for worry and we were confidant it would remain that way.

We did however notice something different in the flood of 2000.

It was the way in which West Moor, our moor, filled up. Taking our usual walks down the bank towards the pumping station we watched the river full to the brim spilling over the banks into the moor. Great sheets of water, stretches of thirty, forty yards in places, cascaded over. Rippling on the grass banks, shimmering in the winter sun, it was beautiful. We'd never seen this happen in quite the same way before, seepage yes, but not like this; as a result the moor seemed to fill more quickly. It was not evident to us at the time but the bank was sinking, compressed by cattle and general wear and tear, always worst in the gateways and it needed maintenance, re-levelling that it was not getting.

Very early in January 2000 we crossed to France, driving down to the south west where Emily, our daughter, was spending a year as a teaching assistant in the small market town of Marmande on the river Garonne as part of her university course. We'd been so absorbed in our own flooded world in Somerset that we were totally unprepared for the destruction and damage we found in France. A few days earlier, hurricane force winds had torn across the north of the country, followed a few days later by the same violent windstorm in the south. Hundreds of signs on the autoroute had been ripped away, service stations blown apart, buying fuel became a real concern; in the Perigeux region, north of Bergerac and the Dordogne, whole forests of oak had been mowed down, roads blocked, detours everywhere. It turned into a marathon journey. In the local paper the next day was the photo of a merchant vessel on the coast carried inland by the storm surge and deposited in a field. It seemed we'd had the rain, but they'd had the wind.

*****

And that seemed the last of our floods. There followed more than a decade of some of the hottest summers, the coldest winters, greater extremes of weather than we'd ever seen before. In 2007 on a flight to Australia I read Tim Flannery's thought-provoking book, *The Weather Makers* and became familiar with such terms as climate change, global warming, the effects of fossil fuels; the threshold of 2 degrees beyond which the world would start to cook. In our own lives it was a time of selling the business, of discovering retirement and new interests, of becoming grandparents.

And always at the centre of it all, Willow Cottage. Home, a place to drop anchor.

And then it was 2012. Year of the London Olympics. Watching Usain Bolt in the Olympic stadium kneel at the start of the 100m heats on Super Saturday with Oliver, my son, and my five-year-old grandson, (£5 entry) actually more interested at that precise moment in searching under the seat to find his Jamaican flag than he was in witnessing the great man fly down the track. 2012, one of the wettest years on the Levels, a year of endless rain, it seemed, and summer flooding. A disastrous summer for farmers on the Levels ruining silage and fodder crops for overwintering animals. In the July, five inches of rain fell and several times that summer West Moor flooded.

In the garden it was the year of the slug. They thrived on the wet and our vegetables. They grew huge and rubbery

and increasingly bold, completely oblivious to the lashings of
slug pellets we scattered around the plants. They could devour
a mature courgette plant in a night or a row of beans. Nightly
I waged war, collecting them by the bucketful, great black and
orange creatures, glutinous and slimy, the size of sausages with
their huge muscular footpads like old gymshoes. I'd hurl them
into the river. In the end, like some horror movie, I began to
think that if I fell over or slipped I'd be found in the veg patch
in the morning, a heap of clean-picked bones.

In Thorney alone, on ground already saturated after
one of the wettest summers, nearly four inches fell in October
2012. And as we sat in our conservatory, our living room
for most of the year, with the rain hammering on the glass
above us, we began to wonder if something wasn't different;
the volume of rain felt heavier, fatter. Monsoon rain. In the
November a further 143 millimetres or 5.6 inches of rain fell
on Thorney, which meant nearly ten inches in two months. By
the last week of November 2012 the river was running very
high, over-spilling the bank on the way down to the pumping
station, flooding our West Moor. It all happened very quickly.
Roads were out, Muchelney cut off, lots of phone calls and
sharing of travel information, people meeting and talking,
'Never seen it so high... never like this before...'

My diary entry of 24th November 2012 however records
no great sign of anxiety, we'd seen all this before, focussing
instead on describing the scene on the moor:

*'Rain on and off all week. Big floods. Not up to 2000 or
1990 but still very extensive. Walked tonight with Poppy,
[our lurcher]. Beautiful afternoon. From the river bank to
One Tree hill, a huge lake. Very still. Mist rising like smoke.
Three quarter moon. Water birds taking over. Clamour of
geese like crowd at football match. Thin wands of willows like
witches' brooms punctuate the water. Just the top bars of gates
showing and a line of poplars. Peewits. But it's not settled
yet; the flood is still shifting, redistributing itself like a great
weight, still moving, settling.*

How things could change. The diary moves on, measuring like a dipstick the changes in mood and situation. From that nonchalant entry to this, a few days later on Wednesday 28th November. It's even headed 'The Great Flood':

'*The worst flood in 60 or 70 years, they say, nothing like this since the bank was raised. Seems ages since I wrote last entry. Never had an inkling then that it would turn into such a drama.*

It rained all Friday night and was wet and drizzly on Saturday, then heavy again. River huge. No sign of hedges, gates on moor, all covered by one great sheet of water. Creeping up Holly's lane. Into the road. By Sunday night beginning to get really worried. Take cars up to Chrissie's – Utta's idea. By Monday work on doors, sealing them with mastic. Great escape was uncovering the drain on the patio to allow the flood to get away. It just got us out of trouble. There was seepage under the flags into the sitting room but one more pump, loaned by Michael in the bungalow, just kept it clear.

Lots of lessons for next time.

Flood is still rising though river is down. Linda was evacuated on Sunday night, the Prof on Monday early. Johnny Leach and all the houses down there, Nigel and Kate, Mike and Jenny Curtis all flooded. Muchelney totally cut off. Liz and Peter flooded at Muchelney Ham. No tractors coming through, just boats and canoes. Today's job, reinforce the front door and borrow a pump from Julian.'

All week the flood kept rising, creeping up the road past our house and up to the hump back bridge. This was different from anything we'd seen before. The flood had always stayed contained by the moor. Never before in our life in the village had it broken out and crossed the road. The rain had stopped, the wind had ceased but like a huge tanker, a great weight adrift, unstoppable, born along by sheer momentum, the flood kept coming, inching up the road to within a whisker, a millimetre of entering the house. Every few hours I'd check with Roddy on the corner; his house was safe but he was very worried about a new outside boiler just installed. Then as it hovered at our doors choosing its moment of entry, the relentless momentum stilled. And stopped.

We had just escaped.

The family and the grandchildren came down for the weekend. We met them at the end of the road, loading the two boys into the boat, 'Sit on the seat, that's it, arms round each other,' as we steered them down the road over the flood to Willow Cottage. Maybe in years to come, when they grow old, in far off places, they'll say to their children or grandchildren, 'I remember years ago, being put in a boat by my grandparents and taken through the floods to their house.' The water in their story will be deeper, much deeper, and it will be a mile at least – not a hundred yards. But it'll make a wonderful story. Their own little people will listen, eyes wide open, inhaling the drama, the danger conjured up by those distant memories.

*****

We'd survived but only just. By the very narrowest of margins we'd stayed dry. Two houses in this end of the village, the two lowest had gone under; many more in the other half of Thorney had flooded. It left us scarred. And scared. Confidence in the impregnability of our home severely shaken. For the first time we saw the shock, the dazed look, on the faces of friends and families flooded, how shattering its effect could be. It rattled the very foundations of our existence, caused huge upheaval in the pattern of normal daily living.

It did though have its lighter moments. John and Lizzie Leach had decamped from their flooded house to their shop and exhibition space across their courtyard, built on higher ground. It was warm and they could cook in there, but there was no loo. Johnny was lamenting this fact when suddenly, on cue, a blue Portaloo floated into view on the flooded road outside. It was grabbed, tethered and set in place. They always did say, 'The Good Lord doth provide.'

However close you've been to flooding, as we had just been, it still gives you no idea of the actual experience of your house being under water. For us the impact of this near miss was soon softened, forgotten by the coming of Christmas and family staying. For those who had flooded however we saw how their lives were turned upside down for months, dislocated, their houses besieged all year by dryers and builders. There was frustration, anger at the EA and authorities who'd barely been seen throughout the whole episode along with increasing calls for dredging the river.

At a village meeting held in Muchelney church the following summer of 2013 the local community met the EA and the IDB (Internal Drainage Board). It began with power point presentations on big screens, graphs, bullet points, images of water spilling over banks. An exercise in damage limitation, the big placebo. When it was thrown open to the floor, the question most often asked from those who'd flooded was, 'So what are you going to do about it?' Always met with soothing replies but always inherent in the response, we felt, was the unspoken answer: 'There's not a lot we can do'. It was never explicit but in the Teflon replies to exasperated questioners the suggestion crept in that we shouldn't complain – the problem was, we were living in the wrong place. And the meeting ended with the prophetic reassurance,

'Don't worry, it'll never happen again. Not in a hundred years.'

*****

For the rest of 2013 rainfall was average, (ten inches less than in 2012), with a delicious long hot summer. Pay-back time. The veggies flourished, barely a slug in sight.

That autumn we were invited for a drink with Liz and Peter Nightingale on the road out of Muchelney. Their house had badly flooded the previous November and was now nearly restored after a long and fraught year of builders and noise. As we chatted to various other guests I found myself in the middle of their sitting room standing beside an oak post that supported the ceiling. To a height of about eighteen inches above the floor the wood was stained dark by floodwater. 'That's a piece of history,' someone said. 'A reminder to future generations.' 'Yes,' another voice added,' that was a one-off. We'll never see that again – never in a hundred years.'

Then the rain began. Hardly noticeable at first because the moors were well drained after a good summer and the river still low but in the month of October Thorney received five inches of rainfall.

On the other side of the world, on November 8th, typhoon Haiyan, one of the most powerful storms ever to hit land, struck the Philippines, killing over six thousand and displacing four million. Within little more than a week an armada of aid was on its way to help the stricken inhabitants.

For us the rainfall paused but in early December a series of major storms battered other parts of the country: the Norfolk coast experienced its worst tidal surge in over 60 years; several houses built on cliffs in East Anglia slipped into the sea. By contrast here in the south west all seemed relatively tranquil with no great cause for alarm. In the week leading up to December 20th there were two inches of rain. Nothing unusual, the river rose as it always did after heavy rain. Just another winter.

But it was not to last. It was as if the weather, having bullied the eastern side of the country for a month, now turned its attention to the south west. In the last ten days of 2013 it rained every day; the river rose, the moor began to fill. Two days before Christmas we took the grandchildren to a pantomime in Yeovil through sheets of rain – nearly two inches fell in twenty four hours. By the time we returned after the show the river had swollen and was across the road in several places. Like the starter's flag, the road to Langport, always the first to go, was beginning to flood. An old friend on his way up from Cornwall to stay that night made numerous detours to reach us, one road after another blocked by flash flooding. In the morning I guided him onto the main A303 for his onward journey unaware that it too had flooded and was impassable.

Around Christmas the rain eased and we were able to forget about the weather, the whole family with the grandchildren gathered together. For daily entertainment we'd walk to inspect the floods. By the weekend before New Year however West Moor across the road was filling fast. I planted a marker stick close to the bank in the orchard by the river. Each time we passed, I was moving it higher and higher again. Deep down I was beginning to worry. We had never seen it like this before.

Then on the last day of the year something very strange happened. We were walking down the river bank; my marker stick had almost vanished. The moor was a wild open sea of floodwater, the sky angry and boiling. More rain on the way. Suddenly I became aware of hundreds of frightened creatures, voles, mice, small mammals everywhere, emerging from cover in the drowning grass of the riverbank, fleeing the flood, scampering onto the rafts of reed and stick blown to the edge to find shelter. Grass snakes, creatures that should have been dormant, hibernating, coiled and slithered amongst them, not hunting but fleeing what they sensed was coming. Their panic was palpable. We felt it too: a great sense of unease as if something strange and terrible was about to happen. Something apocalyptic.

Chapter 3

BATTLE FOR SURVIVAL

JANUARY 1ST 2014

It is late afternoon on New Year's Day. Already getting dark. We are sitting in the kitchen having tea with friends when suddenly there is an urgent banging on the door. Not an inquisitive, friendly knock. No, this is different, urgent, full of alarm. Our neighbour, Glen, his voice breathless, taut with emotion,

'Michael, Utta, just come to tell you, we're moving the cars out, the water's in the road. It's coming up the lane on the corner.' And he is gone, leaving a deep sense of foreboding.

Looking back, that moment, that afternoon on New Year's Day, is the point when normal daily life ended; it's the dotted line between the before and the after. Over the last few days we've been more than usually uneasy and trying to reassure ourselves that we have never flooded before in over thirty years. We have defended this house many times against the flood. Yet it's never begun quite like this before; there's something ominous about its relentless encroachment, the speed with which it has advanced upon us. Almost immediately our friends, Biddy and Paul, who've called in for tea and to catch up on news, rise and take their leave,

'We must go too before we get cut off.' They've brought their cars over and parked one at the Leach pottery. It will be several weeks before we see them again.

We phone friends about half a mile away who live on higher ground on the road to Kingsbury, well out of any flood, to ask if they would let us park on their driveway as we did in November 2012. They are happy for us to do so again. As I drive up there, a dark tongue of water is already spreading into the road from the lane leading to the moor. In the headlights, figures, torches shining on the water, gauging its depth; outside houses, glimpses of fevered activity, scrabbling with sandbags, moving vehicles.

I can feel my heart thumping. In my head I'm beginning to make lists, furious with myself that all the things I planned to have ready after the last time, I haven't done. There didn't seem the urgency, life just slipped by, it was so easy to believe it wouldn't happen again, 'never in a hundred years'.

Top of the list is to get hold of our new pump man, Nigel Talbot, for some more pumps, then bar and seal the front and side doors and start raising furniture. Even as I walk back from parking the vehicle, the water has crept further up the road towards our house. It's like some dark creature moving stealthily with deadly intent. What is most troubling is that it's moving at a rate far faster than the flood of 2012.

I manage to get hold of Nigel and he promises to come next morning, bringing more pumps. That at least is a huge relief and raises our spirits. That evening we start to prepare defences. By some miracle I find in the jumble of my shed the planks we used last time to board up the main door to the lowest part of the house, screwing and sealing them with mastic to the door frame – much more effective than sand bags, and a lesson learned last time from Glen, our carpenter neighbour. We then start to raise the furniture in the little sitting room, behind the sealed door. If I'd done what I'd meant to do, I should have had a stack of blocks to hand ready to use, instead I stumble about in the garden, only grateful for the head torch I was given for Christmas, foraging for bricks and blocks, most of which are sodden and hairy with moss. It's started to rain heavily again and the wind has got up.

Utta has the inspired idea of using the bricks from the bookshelf upstairs that runs the length of the wall on the landing; each plank shelf is supported by three or four bricks, all clean and dry. It's our first act of serious dismantling. We double stack books and rob the bricks to raise the big sofa, given to us years ago by my sister. It's a very long one, very comfy, with room enough to seat at least three people; guests have often slept on it when the house has been full and when I used to get back from the river in the elver season in the small hours of the night I often used it as a temporary bed so as not to wake Utta who would herself soon be off to her nursing at the crack of dawn. It has history, this sofa, like so much furniture, so many belongings in a home: it's an old friend, part of the family.

'Is two blocks enough, what do you think?'

'Oh yes. Easily, it's never going to get that deep.' How little do we know.

To save on blocks and time it seems a good idea to balance a second sofa on top, along with an arm chair. Anything else, the lighter stuff, rugs and light furniture, we take upstairs to one of the bedrooms. I catch myself thinking, this is so strange. Unreal. I can't believe this is happening, it's as if I'm moving in a dream.

Before going to bed, I inspect the situation outside with Poppy, our black lurcher. She is not a water dog and crosses the puddles in the drive with exaggerated hops in an attempt to keep her toes dry. There's already about an inch covering the road outside, but the drive and the back of our house are still relatively dry. I check the pump in the French drain by the back door and though the sump is full, it's not overflowing. This might be as bad as it gets but somehow I fear the worst,

I've never seen it encroach so swiftly. We stand on the top of the river bank together and survey the scene. The rain has eased but the river is huge and swollen, swirling past us in the dark. Every now and then it makes a sound like a gulp or a belch. From upstream there is the boom of the water through the mill weir. The field opposite, where the bank is lower, is completely flooded.

Years ago on such a night as this, dark and moonless, the river in spate might well have triggered a late run of eels, adult silvers, migrating down river out to sea for their return journey across the Atlantic to their spawning grounds in the Sargasso. I remember once in the early years of the smokery going to collect eels from a river keeper on the Avon south of Salisbury; it was blowing a gale and every road I tried was flooded or blocked. When eventually I reached him he had caught nearly a ton the previous night, so many that I was obliged to make a return journey the following day. There are still eels in the Parrett – there may be some running now – though their numbers are diminished.

The height of the river, held behind the bank, is now on a level with the top of our kitchen windows; in the early days this used to make us very nervous but no longer as we have grown to have faith in this bank, it's a hefty piece of work, broad-backed, some ten metres wide at its base and it has always held. What's changed now is that the flood danger is not, as in the past, coming from the river on this side of the house but from the moor over the road. And what is really worrying is the knowledge that about half a mile down river it will now be seriously 'overtopping' in an uncontrolled fashion, pouring over the bank into the moor, filling it like a huge bowl higher and higher until it reaches the lane, the road and our houses.

To make matters worse, tonight, some fourteen miles downriver is a massive high tide, 5.3 metres – nearly 18 feet – above sea level. (Our house is only 25 feet above sea level.) For nearly an hour and a half either side of high water, the Parrett at Bridgwater, now swollen by the Tone, the Yeo and the Isle that have joined it along its course to the sea, will be blocked, 'tide locked', unable to discharge this huge volume of flood water into the estuary. It can only back up.

As an old elver fishermen once put it,

'Can't get out see, Mike, that there flood water; tis as if ee's all bunged up like.' And he was right in a way: it's all a matter of digestion.

As we take in the scene, Pop sits quivering beside me, nose twitching then looks at me sideways in the dark as if to say, 'Can we go in now?'

At night, we sleep with the windows open, jamming them with my father's old gardening socks to stop them from rattling in the wind. We might just as well be sleeping outside were it not for a good duvet and we like it that way. We used to sleep under an old feather bed, which belonged to Utta's parents and would have served well up a mountain it was so warm. That was before it started to leak feathers and fine down which got up your nose as you slept. I always like to look out into the night before getting into bed; tonight the sky is full of great, dark clouds like battleships, wind rising. More rain is on the way.

Drifting in and out of fitful sleep, I can hear the roar of the river through the mill.

MORNING – THURSDAY JANUARY 2ND

Awake early, taut as a drum, it's barely light. Utta still asleep. Sense something different: an unfamiliar light playing on the ceiling by the window. Getting up, I realise that it's the reflection from outside: the orchard and lower part of the garden have flooded. Booted up, I do the rounds. Rain gauge shows there's been nearly an inch of rain. Water now just up to the top of the pavement by the road and starting to creep up the drive. Meanwhile the puddles on the drive from the night before have joined up to become sheets of water. Pop

comes with me, lifting her toes pointedly through the water,
crouching to pee with one back leg raised to keep it dry. The
river is as high as I've ever seen it, within a foot from the top
of our bank. I place a stick as a marker. The bank opposite
has vanished, overwhelmed, the field become a lake stretching
to the line of the far hedge; already the gulls are gathering at
its edge.

The pump from the French drain is working but the delivery
hose is a length of one inch plastic pipe delivering a pathetic thin
flow, not even a jet, woefully inadequate in the circumstances.
Then with a shock I realise the main sump in the centre of
the turning circle is brim full. Hauling the big pump out of
the well is a horrible job as it spews foul water all over me. I
can see it's dead, lifeless, and has caused the water to back up
into the drains around the house. Even without a flood, there's
something deeply disturbing about blocked drains; not being
free to empty baths, flush loos, use washing machines.

At this moment, like the cavalry to the rescue, Nigel
Talbot arrives in his Land Rover. A big man with Breton
moustaches, wearing enormous steel capped wellies, he's just
the person you want in an emergency, quiet, confident and
entirely professional. His vehicle is immaculate, gleaming,
fitted with spotlights and winches and in the back a complete
workshop, as neat as a pin, with racks of tools, pumps, hoses, and
specialist kit. We survey the situation together. He knows the
site well from the flood of 2012. Pulling on rubber gloves like
a surgeon he sets to work. In under an hour he has examined
and condemned the pump I've just hauled up, swapped it for
two larger ones, both pumping through 3' pipes directly into
the river like twin canon. He works swiftly and rhythmically.
We bring him cups of tea and praise. The pumps are beginning
to have an effect already. The level in the inspection drain by
the house is beginning to drop. It's infinitesimal yet as you
watch, millimetre by millimetre, the level is being clawed back
revealing first one brick, then another. The water is going into

reverse. I call to Utta to share my excitement. It's thrilling stuff. The enemy is in retreat. We're beating the bastard.

Strange, comical almost, how life at this moment has become focussed entirely on tiny changes in water level in a brick drain but this is what flooding does to you and it can mean the difference between survival or disaster.

It's at times like these I feel I'm almost back in the old elver days, the bumper years of the 1970s and 1980s when the flood of catches were coming in to our holding site faster than I could get them to market: the same nightmare of being overwhelmed. Then it was from elvers. Now it's flood water.

Nigel leaves, on his way to another job, 'Keep all this lot until things sort themselves out and we can settle up later, just give me a shout if you need me.'

Inside, Utta is taking precautions, carrying stuff upstairs in between fielding the phone which rings constantly, calls from family, from friends who have been listening to the news of the flooding, checking to see we're all right, 'so far so good', she reassures them. On the local grapevine we learn that Muchelney is fast becoming cut off, the Langport road has gone, you can just get through to Drayton, but that'll soon be out, the road to Thorney is covered but still just passable, so and so is getting very nervous. And so it goes on. The flood increasing its grip.

MID-MORNING – THURSDAY JANUARY 2ND

We've never seen it this bad before, never seen it envelop us all so quickly; it dwarfs the flood of 2012. And yet we're still optimistic we can keep it out of the house; at least we are holding it at bay.

Mid-morning. We decide to stop for a break. We are sitting in the conservatory, Utta's just made coffee. It's delicious to sit down and pretend to be normal for a moment. We both realise we're knackered, something to do with the adrenalin, the nervous energy. We chat about family and news gathered from the phone calls.

Then suddenly the power goes off. And silence. Everything stops. We phone around: is it just us, or is everyone affected? It's everyone. The whole area south of Thorney. I rush outside onto the river bank to check the pumps and of course they've stopped. Already the small gains that we'd made are going into reverse, the water beginning to climb back up the brickwork in the inspection drain. Under the stairs, I remember, is stowed a small Honda generator that we used to use for draining ponds and tanks. It was one of the things on my list to have it serviced and ready on stand-by. Miraculously, though it's not been used for years, its starts on the second pull. Better still it has fuel and just enough power to run the smallest pump. We're still losing ground but it helps a little.

Next I'm on the phone to Nigel. By a stroke of luck, I catch him as he is coming back from another job; he will divert to his workshop to pick up a generator and another pump. He'll be with us in a couple of hours. I now realise I'm going to need fuel for the generators. A quick round of the neighbours, sloshing up the road in my wellies, produces five plastic containers which together with our own should give us enough. Leaving Utta, I wade out again to pick up the car parked on dry land, and drive to the nearest garage in Martock – mercifully, the road is open. It is there that I meet Peter and Liz Nightingale also buying fuel for their pumps which they use to defend their property at Muchelney Ham, on the southern edge of Muchelney village. They are old hands at this, they flooded in November 2012 and they've only just got their house straight again. For them it's been a stressful year of insurance, builders and chaos, yet they seem remarkably chirpy and cheerful. I feel their concern for us, fellow victims, they know how it feels. Curiously the flood hasn't reached them yet, maybe it won't. Last time it was different, they were almost the first to suffer. From one event to the next, there seems to be no set pattern. We swap news, they have numbers of family staying over from Australia; I sense this might be both a help and a hindrance. We say our farewells; like two small craft in the ocean meeting by chance, both keenly aware of each other's difficulties and distress; a hug and we part, each to our own battles. Realise with surprise I'm quite wobbly and emotional. Drive home with seven cans of fuel.

Note that in the time I've been away the water is now well into the garden and with it a veritable armada of bobbing cider apples, windfalls from the small orchards on the edge of the moor, pushed up the drive by the bow wave of passing vehicles. They seem terribly excited to find somewhere else to explore – this is much more interesting than being left on the grass to rot – and they are already examining the veg garden, Utta's flower beds. Like visitors allowed into a property normally off-limits, you can almost hear them,

'Oh look at them there leeks! And over there, they flower beds. Must be a sight in season. Don't think much of his sprouts though.'

Nigel is back with a large petrol generator with capacity to drive both the pumps he delivered in the morning. He also brings another big pump, this one petrol-driven. And with them more hose, immaculately coiled in the back of the truck, unwound in sections that clip together. We place them strategically in the various sumps and drains like soldiers in gun emplacements directing artillery. The noise is terrible with the banging of the petrol engines. They all need filling about every two and a half hours. Gradually the momentum lost through the power cut is regained, the water level in the inspection drain just beginning to recede.

After he leaves, the rest of the day is a blur. At some stage as it's getting dark, the water enters not only across the lawn, but under the garden wall along the front of the conservatory, creeping onto the flag stones outside the front door, the lowest part. It's like being attacked on several fronts. If unchecked, I know this will go straight in through the front door despite the boards screwed and sealed across it. They won't survive a bigger assault.

Then suddenly I remember something that helped save us last time. Under one of the flag stones outside the front door is the inspection chamber for the drainage from the kitchen and bathroom upstairs. The drain is perfectly placed and deep enough for a small pump. It will act as a sort of forward unit, a first line of defence, intercepting the floodwater and delivering it straight to the river.

The only trouble is the flag stone lid to the drain is reinforced with concrete and is immensely heavy. Calling for Utta's help, and with the aid of metal bars, shovels and brute force, we manage to lever it up and prop it open like a car bonnet, allowing enough space for a small pump to drop inside. Rummaging around – all this I had meant to have had ready prepared – we manage to cobble together just enough hose to reach the river – some thirty metres away. The power is back on at last so we're able to feed the cable out through the kitchen window. Almost straightaway the pump settles down, gulping the flood water before it has time even to think about entering the house. It makes reassuring sucking sounds like a baby given its bottle at bedtime. Our spirits rise.

By now the river end of the garden has the look of dereliction, an abandoned industrial site, half submerged. A tangle of electric cables, suspended like bunting to keep them clear of the water, extension reels under plastic bags, hoses from the pumps trail across the drive and lawn like great rat tails to discharge over the bank into the river.

With so many pumps I have run out of hoses, so have to cobble them together from assorted lengths of old plastic pipe shoved one inside the other. The problem is that having run out of proper connectors the pumped water tends to escape through the joints when it reaches the sharp incline of the bank and flows back into the garden. To overcome this, I have to raise the pipes gradually in a gentle gradient, first over an upturned bucket, then onto the wheelbarrow, then picnic bench and finally a stepladder to gain the height of the top of the bank to allow it to flow the last bit by gravity into the river.

It's very primitive, very Heath Robinson, but it works.

And so to bed.

Up again around midnight to top up the new petrol pump, re-set the alarm for its next refuelling.

2AM FRIDAY JANUARY 3RD

Suddenly I'm wide awake. It's 2am. I lie there listening. Something's wrong, something's different, I know it. There's silence, that's what's wrong; no sucking sounds from the pump outside below our window. As long as I could hear them, I felt we were safe. It can only mean the water level has risen − considerably. Throw on some clothes and quietly without waking Utta make my way down through the house, shabby as an old coat, still warm and redolent of Christmas and the little boys. I pass their boxes of toys, the odd piece of lego left on the carpet, knobbly underfoot; into the kitchen, warmed by the Rayburn puttering as ever like a geriatric; hear the clock ticking, the occasional creak of the house, all those familiar sounds. Like a person breathing, an old friend much loved.

Then pausing for a moment I slowly open the door through to the little sitting room with its step down into the lowest part of the house and turn on the light.

What I see makes my heart pound, it's our worst fear: the whole floor is glistening wet, barely half an inch deep, but it's in. We are flooding. I feel sick. I watch it. Stealthily, it invades, coming not just from the door but welling up from beneath, darkening the grouting between the flagstones, and all so gently, ever so gently. Like evil. Uninvited, invading our space, our lives.

Outside the wind has dropped, the sky full of stars. I see the rising water has overwhelmed the pump outside the kitchen and the others too. All are working flat out but they can make no headway against the sheer volume of water from the flood.

I feel sure though that if only we could get hold of one or two more pumps we could still tip the balance and turn the tide as we did the last time. The river has dropped a little by about a foot, at least it might not be spilling over into the moor lower down. The trouble is that it's far too early to ring anyone now so I go back upstairs. I'll wait till first thing in the morning before asking around.

> As I can't get back to sleep and not wanting to wake Utta, I go into Emily's room, the bed still made up from Christmas, turn on the radio and listen to the Fifth Ashes Test live from Sydney where for a brief spell we seem to be in the ascendant. The Aussies are in to bat and are 97 for 5, Broad has just taken another wicket. The commentary, the familiar voices, the drama under the sun twelve thousand miles away helps to take my mind off the grim present. I must have dozed off for when I wake again the Aussies are back in control with Haddin and Smith whacking us all over the ground.

FRIDAY MORNING, JANUARY 3RD

Soon after seven, I take a deep breath and phone the Temperleys at Burrow Hill Cider. Diana answers, her voice full of sleep. She'll let Julian know. He calls back a short while later. No need to come up to the farm, he can bring the pump down to his father's house around eight when he's meeting someone, probably an insurance man. I can pick it up from there. When we unload the pump and hose from the back of his car, they come with a strong cidery smell. Thorney House is lower than ours and is on the side of the road nearest the moor. The house, home to Julian's father, Professor Temperley, is already flooded and abandoned. Julian and the insurance man are inspecting the damage. I can hear the slosh of their boots and their voices echoing. It's a grim sight in there, dark, devastated and lifeless. Water laps at the furniture. The professor and Deirdre, his faithful carer, have been evacuated to a safe place. As we might wonder at the height of great floods, so too we are awed by a great age achieved: the professor is in his late nineties, just short of a hundred, born in 1915 during the First World War, the year of Gallipoli and the 2nd Battle of Ypres; he is a link to another age, living history.

An hour later Nigel Talbot is back to us with one more big pump.

'That's all of them,' he says with a smile, 'You've got everything from the yard now!'

He parks on the only piece of gravel still dry on our drive. He cannot stay long, it's over a foot deep in the road and rising. He sets up the new pump and the borrowed one from Julian. Together we place them in the most effective positions and reappraise the layout of our defences, swapping a bigger pump to deal with the water in front of the kitchen. We now have a total of seven pumps and calculate that with all of them going full bore we are discharging nearly a hundred cubic metres of water an hour into the river. However when viewed from the top of the bank, the water swirling by, the garden almost submerged, this impressive statistic withers into insignificance.

'I must be off before I get trapped, see you when I see you. Good luck.' And he is gone.

It is beginning to rain heavily again. The water in the old part of the house is now about two inches deep, yet with the extra reinforcements acquired today, we are holding it. In military terms we've retired to higher ground to fight on. The old part is six inches lower: if we can hold it there, the rest of the house can still be saved.

The rest of the day passes in an endless round of checking the pumps, trying to squeeze the very best out of each of them. They need constant watching, for every now and then the intake where they draw the water becomes clogged by the increasing amount of flood debris, fine duckweed, sticks, roots being borne across the moor the by the south-westerly. This debris is like the rougher elements of an invading army, the hangers-on, the chancers. Meanwhile the battle between the advancing flood and the speed with which the pumps can hurl it into the river is finely balanced. I quickly learn that if I stop a pump to swap it with another, or to clear an intake, something that may take ten minutes, the flood seizes the initiative and all our gains are lost. Changes are costly and have to be carefully weighed up in advance.

Meanwhile it's grinding work hampered by wet-weather gear. One of the worst tasks is when I need to check a big pump, hauling it fifteen feet up from the depths of the cess pit sump. As it comes up it inevitably snags with the hose or cable of another and I end up hauling two, sometimes three pumps to the surface, a huge weight, all spewing foul water. Valuable time is then lost disentangling them. In the dark, bent over to work, my wool hat with its head torch attached keeps sliding off my head over my eyes and I can't see. If it wasn't so frustrating, the sight of it must be hilarious. Instead I vent my anger by loosing off volleys of foul expletives into the night sky aimed at the flood, the EA and life in general.

It's a slog every step of the way, I feel like Sisyphus condemned by the gods to roll his rock to the top of the hill. These are the low points. But now and then when I've cleared a pump or repositioned it to good effect, and the water level shrinks back into the inspection drain, it's worth every ounce of effort. One of those Hollywood moments when you expect to hear the music swell as the forces of good break through at last. Only this is the real world and the water gives no sign of relenting. This is a flood of a size and scale we've never seen before.

At intervals through the day there's a shout from a doorway, 'Cuppa tea?' And we meet and hug and catch up with snippets of conversation, exchange of news.

'I've put all that stuff upstairs in the boy's room.'

'The new pump's working well. But the river's up again.'

'Your sister phoned to see how we were. And Em too. She's well.'

'All those bloody apples trying to get inside.'

Each break is a tiny oasis of peace, some sense of normality, an escape from the invading chaos.

While I struggle outside Utta works tirelessly indoors, raising onto blocks furniture too heavy to move elsewhere, carrying upstairs what she can. It's only when you flood that you realise just how much lives on the floor of a room: apart from the obvious carpets and rugs, there are all those lamps and tables and chairs and chests and cupboards. And when you can no longer use this precious space that you take for granted, you have to find a home for it all, and fast. Your mind goes blank – it's like having the removals lorry turn up before you're ready. On Thursday – yesterday, it seems like an age ago – we started putting furniture onto blocks, the bricks on their sides, wrapped in paper so as not to dirty the carpet. We've grown up now. That was starters, this is the main course. We don't bother with that anymore. We're onto the third layer of bricks now, the carpet's already dead under two inches of water, our first real casualty. Well, we say, we were never very fond of it, it always showed the dirt.

Besides moving furniture, Utta is almost as busy answering the phone. The calls come thick and fast, people phoning to see how we are; conversation often runs along the same lines, 'Oh hello, how are you? No, we're OK. Flooded in the lower part but the main is still dry. Fingers crossed. Thanks for ringing. Lots of love...' They're a welcome interruption to the grimness of the flood, and are full of genuine sympathy. You can almost sense the stab of shock in the voice on the line when they hear that we are already partly under water. 'Oh I'm so sorry,' as they absorb that truth, perhaps visualising it in their own home. And always, 'If there's anything we can do, just let us know, meals, baths, washing. Just phone.' And they mean it.

Dog tired, we're in bed by eight. I'm up again at midnight and again at three to refill the petrol pump. According to our rain gauge, well over an inch of rain, 27mm, has fallen in the last 24 hours; more than that will have fallen on the hills and all of it will be on its way down within the next few hours. The river is huge, back up to my marker, nearly to the top of the bank. Tonight another high tide at Bridgwater, well over 17 feet, and as high again in the morning. This means that for hours at a time this vast mass of floodwater will be blocked, prevented from escaping out to sea.

Slowly we are drowning.

As I stand on the bank in the dark, the boom of the mill up-river, an owl hoots, a long quavering note, answered by another. A pair of tawnies hunting. They live in the trees over the road at the end of the Temperley's garden; probably after the mice and rats moving to take refuge in sheds, houses, driven to shelter by the water. The soft note of the owl is somehow soothing; another world out there, outside the flood.

SATURDAY MORNING – JANUARY 4TH

I go down to check the situation. In the old part of the house, the water has risen to just two inches below the level of the kitchen. Poppy looks distinctly nervous. Usually in the mornings when I come down to make the tea, we have a ritual cuddle, she leans against me and talks as I rub her chest and undercarriage. When I let her out she bounds into the garden, barking furiously, before straddling for a pee. Then nose to ground like a hoover, body stiff with indignation, she tracks at speed the scent of cat or badger or fox that may have passed in the night, 'How dare they!' accelerating across the lawn like a missile in a sweeping curve up onto the bank into the neighbour's garden and is gone. Only to return a few minutes later in much better mood, problem clearly sorted, and trots amiably back into the house for her breakfast. It's her morning patrol, a check on all boundaries. But not today. As we stand at the door to the conservatory, the water is just below the sill, she looks at me as if to say, 'No thank you, not going out in that' and goes back to bed.

The garden has become a lake, already too deep in places for wellies. I curse myself for not having bought the waders that were on my list of things to do. The pumps are still flat out but like some giant session of arm wrestling they are gradually being overwhelmed one by one by the sheer weight and volume of floodwater. We make one last effort. Utta sweeps with a broom again and again along the narrow outhouse floor, creating a great surge of water that rolls out of the back door to the area of the inspection drain where we've repositioned the two biggest pumps. Using the step into the kitchen as her marker, it seems to be working. 'Michael, we're gaining. We're gaining. It's going down. Only two inches now.' For a while we're buoyed by a great rush of euphoria and throw ourselves back to the fight. We keep going, brushing and sweeping for the next two hours. But by 10am the water has climbed to the level of the kitchen floor, spreading unstoppable into the rest of the house. Both exhausted, we meet for a conference.

'What do you think, shall we turn them off?'

It's a terrible decision to make, to throw in the towel. To surrender. But there's some inexorable momentum about this flood, it's still coming up and you sense there's a lot more to come. In effect by pumping, we're taking on the whole flooded moor. We haven't a chance.

It's like a death sentence. I go out and one by one very reluctantly switch off all seven pumps. If they were human I'd feel like thanking them for their service, I'd express my gratitude for their valiant efforts. Pin medals. All of a sudden the garden falls silent. I relish the peace. Unexpectedly, we feel not distress or shock, but a huge wave of relief. We did our best, we fought and we lost. I think it probably helped to have flooded in two halves: the sight of the water covering the floor in the early hours of Friday was the worst thing I think I've ever seen, but it helped to inure us, prepare us for the flooding of the main house. We hug. 'That's it, we're flooded, but we're gonna be alright.'

'At least', as Utta says, 'There's no one shooting at us.'
And I don't have to get up in the night anymore to refill
that sodding petrol pump.

Chapter 4

ADAPTING

SATURDAY JANUARY 4TH

One of the first phone calls this morning is from my brother, Alastair, who lives in Wiltshire. He and the rest of the family have been in touch every day. I tell him we're flooded and down the line can sense his stunned shock.

'Is there anything we can do?'

'Yes, two things: do you think you could you get us some waders and more important, do you think you could have Pop until we're through this? She's getting very worried, very nervous. I don't think she can handle the flood.'

Instantly, without hesitation, the answer comes back, 'Yes of course. No problem. Give me about three hours.' It is typical of him, solid as a rock, generous of spirit, my brother coming to the rescue. We agree that he'll phone when he gets to the edge of the village and we will take Pop up to meet him.

I'm just wondering how I'm going to do this – she doesn't like swimming, too cold, and like most dogs, hates being carried, always wriggling to get free – when I spot my old boat up on the bank under the trees. It's a small fibre-glass dinghy with wooden trim, about seven feet long, broad and very stable, just light enough to carry and it was ideal for setting nets in my eeling days. It has a certain feminine elegance, a beauty of shape like a leaf. I bought it in the late 1970s from father-and-son fishermen who used to set nets to catch eels in the Fleet, that body of lagoon-like water near Abbotsbury on the Dorset coast. Each spring during the elver season they'd drive up to the Parrett in Somerset using their boat to cross the river to fish good spots inaccessible to most. At night they'd often sleep out on the bank under the boat that they propped up on a stick. The old man was called Dick, tall and skinny as a heron, with a red scarf round his neck, tough as old boots; he could have walked straight out of Stevenson's *Treasure Island*. It was his son who made the boats out fibreglass from a mould. I was so impressed I commissioned one, it cost a hundred pounds, but I never regretted it. Sadly she has been neglected, the hull covered in leaves and vegetation, the woodwork beginning to rot. But cleaning her off, dragging her into the floodwater now covering the entire garden, she floats and seems rejuvenated by her immersion. I've long since lost her oars but I intend to use her more like a floating shopping trolley which can be pushed along, and for passengers the thwart, the seat, is still sound enough – just.

Soon after my conversation with Alastair and after digging out the boat, we spot the tall figure of Tim, our local electrician, on the opposite bank now being used as a walkway to get round the flood to reach houses this end of the village. In all the drama of the past few days I've been dimly aware of the potentially disastrous encounter between live electrics in the house and the floodwater but have had no time to give it any real thought. There is now a very real danger of being electrocuted. I know nothing about electrics except that they're best treated with extreme caution. Most of the plugs at floor level around the house will very soon be under water. We hail him from the river bank and by a stroke of luck he is free to come over.

Tim is from the village of Kingsbury just a mile up the road, a tall, bespectacled, quietly-spoken young man.

He wears voluminous, many-pocketed overalls in which he normally has enough of the tools needed for most of the jobs he is called to do at short notice. Seemingly laid back, he has a slightly disturbing habit of turning to talk to you while engaged in probing – what seems to us – deadly live wires with his test screwdriver almost as nonchalantly as if he were pruning roses. He is in fact very careful and competent, happy to take on anything from moving a plug in the kitchen to providing three-phase power for a wedding. One of a number of young men much involved in organising events for the local community, all voluntarily.

'We need to make you safe, that's the first thing,' he says after a preliminary inspection. And sets to work by knocking out the circuit to all the sockets in the house. Examining the fuse box further, he says,

'That's good, we can keep all your lights. They're on a separate circuit.' It's like having a wizard handing out treats from his magic box of goodies. 'And,' he adds, 'you can keep your immersion upstairs – that's on a separate circuit too.' This is very good news for though we might not have any heating we can at least have a hot bath and then leap into bed.

'Is there any way you could give us just one plug to use?' I ask.

In answer, he locates a redundant double socket from outside which he wires into the supply for the electric oven, set well above water level. Into this we can now plug a kettle or a toaster as required. More important into the second socket can be plugged a 50 metre extension cable which we trail upstairs to use for whatever's needed up there. We feel better now, safer and much reassured. We note too that the gas top in the kitchen still functions though the supply line from the bottle outside is well underwater. Somehow one of the bricks from when we were raising the cooker has slipped so that it now leans at a rakish angle like a pirate on one leg; from now on it's a bit like cooking on gimbals at sea.

The water is now spreading right through the house

and rising all the time. The urgency to move stuff upstairs has increased dramatically. To begin with we moved things merely as a sensible precaution, believing still it could never happen, that it would reach its peak and then subside like last time. That was just two days ago. Now with every hour it's deeper, challenging furniture, cupboards, sofas that all seemed well out of its reach. We work in different rooms to cover as much ground as we can: Utta wraps plates and crockery in newspaper in the kitchen then packs them into boxes, as if we are about to move house, which, it dawns on me suddenly, we are in a way. Not far, only upstairs.

I start work in my old office, a small room off the hall, not much bigger than a walk-in cupboard. It has many memories for such a small space. I used to sit at one end at the large Victorian desk of polished veneer, now rather the worse for wear, it is slightly too high for good back posture but has useful deep drawers either side of the foot well. It came from my father's office at home when he retired in the mid-1950s to the northern edge of Dartmoor where, amongst many other things, he ran his own small business growing Christmas trees. So it has good pedigree and we have shared much together, this desk and I. In the back of the upper drawers I used to find small shreds of tobacco from where Dad kept his baccy pouch; I can still even catch its faint aroma. Strange how it takes a flood to focus on belongings like this piece of furniture, to remind ourselves of their sentimental value and how they are so much part of our past, our history.

I've become very fond of this room, however unsuitable it may have been as an office. It has been a good place to work, my space where I could shut myself away, a bit like a cave or cell with few distractions. Just pictures of the family and of long-departed tribal elders around me. I have done a lot of thinking, planning, writing – and worrying – in here. In the winter the room would get so cold that I used to get inside a sleeping bag to keep warm – a most effective draught excluder – though it meant hopping like a sack race if someone came to the door. Just last year, I moved computer and files to the new office desk and shelves I built across the hall. So it has now become a storeroom, back office, shelves of reference books, shelves of Utta's homemade jams, seeds for the veg garden, somewhere to put all those things we can never find a home for. It's still used but I no longer sit and work in here for which I feel sad, guilty for having forsaken it like an old friend you don't make time to see any more.

As I stand in here reminiscing I suddenly notice the land line into the house, which runs down the wall and across the hall floor, is under water. I hastily disconnect the phones and also see that the computer tower sitting beneath the desk with all its ugly plugs and wires in my new office is also about to drown and needs moving. This means that our only form of communication is now by mobile phone. This is very unusual for us. Normally our mobiles are turned on only in emergency and quite often they are one of the things we've lost and are searching for: optimistic friends, unaware that we are technologically stunted, leave messages for us that we sometime discover weeks later when the messages they left, often irritable ones like, 'Where are you? We're waiting outside the shop,' have long become irrelevant.

By now the water is beginning to reach the bottom of the filing cabinet and the drawers of the desk in the old office. I extract them one by one like teeth and start carrying them upstairs; later, I promise myself, when things have calmed down I'll go through them and get rid of 'stuff'.

*****

Then something extraordinary happens. I'm half way up the stairs with one of the drawers when my eye falls on the folder on top marked 'Walk out of Burma – Mum's letters'. Over seventy years ago in central Burma, following the Japanese invasion, my mother was given one hour to pack and leave her house and all her belongings. I am suddenly struck by the parallel events: our enforced abandonment of our home – if only to decamp upstairs – echoing, though trivial by comparison, her exodus out of Burma all those years ago. What is also extraordinary is that I should come across this reminder of family history at this very moment, for I haven't looked in the drawer, not even opened it, for well over a year.

She was there because my father, like so many Scots with an adventuring spirit, had chosen to make his life abroad in the Far East and, apprenticed to an overseas trading company, was sent out to Burma in 1926, about as far as he could get from his home in Edinburgh. They had met whilst he was on home leave and had become engaged. They were married in 1938, in Colombo, capital of Ceylon, as it was then called.

By then my father was working for the Bombay Burma Trading Corporation, extracting teak from the jungles, selectively felling only mature trees and using elephants to drag the logs, once dried, to collection points where they could be floated down the great rivers, the Chindwin and Irrawaddy, to the saw mills in Rangoon; the timber in great demand for ships, bridges, all kinds of construction. Looking after often a hundred square miles of forest with his own assistants and teams of elephants, speaking the local language fluently, he loved the life lived out under canvas for months at a time, returning to base during the rainy season. After their honeymoon my mother joined him in his work. On the very first day of their tour they came face to face with a wild elephant, a big bull, very angry, blocking their path, threatening to charge. It could have been a very short marriage, for this was an extremely dangerous situation. My father fired his shotgun into the air and to their great relief the great beast turned and lumbered off into the forest.

My mother shared his life in the jungle and used to speak of it with great fondness, describing their routine of early starts before light, the crisp clean air for they were often high in the hills; best of all she loved watching the elephants after a day's work wallowing in the river, hosing themselves down with their trunks. Camp would be set up ahead of them and food would be ready. At night the two of them would eat at a little table by a camp fire. Wonderfully romantic and certainly a very happy time in their lives.

In the afternoons, while my father worked on paperwork my mother wrote letters home. Fortunately my grandparents living in Cornwall kept them. Reading them again now, down on my knees on the landing, is like being directly in her presence for she wrote as she talked; I can hear her voice as I read her clear, easy-to-read hand writing, blue ink on the thin airmail sheets. There are few crossings out, just the flow of news and descriptions, sometimes with a phrase or expression redolent of the time, 'it was topping.' Letters to and from Europe took about a month to six weeks each way.

In late 1940 they were due home leave but unable to return to England because of the war in Europe, they flew instead with my sister, just a baby, by flying boat to Australia. The journey took six days as they made their leisurely way from Rangoon to Singapore and so on through the Dutch East Indies stopping in Batavia and Surabaya before on to Australia. In Singapore they stayed at the Raffles Hotel of which she writes in a letter home, '...after dinner we danced which was marvellous fun. They have a big ballroom and their own band. It was packed with army, navy and air force.' Twice a day the flying boat came down to refuel and at night in harbour they went ashore to their hotel. The food on board was superb and there was still that sense of unhurried travel: if you missed the view of the volcano or the island reef the pilot simply went round again to give you another look.

In Darwin, after their evening meal at the hotel ashore, my father put their shoes outside the door of their room to be cleaned – as one did in those days. In the morning when he opened the door to collect them, he was surprised to find the shoes hadn't been cleaned. Instead there was a note shoved inside one of them. It read laconically,

'Clean your own bloody shoes!'

It was my parents' first encounter with the wonderful

Aussie sense of fierce independence. They thought it was hilarious and it passed into family parlance. In fact they loved Australia and my mother wrote, 'I have never come across such kindness as out here, every single person you meet seems kinder than the last.'

Outside their world, things were moving with devastating swiftness. The Japanese attack on Pearl Harbour came in December 1941, the fall of Singapore in February 1942, the invasion of Burma soon followed. Japanese troops flooded into the country sweeping north, eyes set on invading India. My father had been posted to Mawlaik in central Burma on the Chindwin river to manage a large area of teak forest. Even before the invasion, the company had carried out its own precautionary planning for the evacuation overland into India of its staff and their families. A route had been reccied that had never been tried before: it involved crossing some of the most inhospitable terrain, over mountains on very narrow trails using elephants to carry kit, baggage and children. The initial report was pessimistic: it couldn't be done. But the rapid Japanese advance gave no choice.

*****

So it was that on February 23rd 1942, a week after the fall of Singapore, my mother, with my sister aged two, together with 37 woman and children, set out from Mawlaik under the leadership of a senior Forest Manager, Geoff Bostock, in a caravan of 56 elephants carrying kit and stores, along with cooks, coolies, servants and nannies. It was extremely well-organised. They were allowed just one suitcase and a bedroll. The children, my sister amongst them, were put in 'doolies', a sort of canvas cot slung on poles and carried by coolies or on the backs of the elephants. For the first nine days from Mawlaik to Temu on the Assam border, the going was relatively easy. Called at 5.30, they would set off in the dark after a hasty cup of tea and some porridge gobbled in the midst of rolling up bed rolls, screaming children, trumpeting elephants, cursing men and coolies. They then marched for an hour before retiring behind bushes, then on again until the next campsite which they usually reached by about midday.

Though their progress was slow, only five or six miles a day to begin with, but working up to ten, they were very well provisioned with live ducks and chickens carried in baskets by the coolies and enough vegetables to last the trek. They slept six to a tent with only one small lamp. Dinner was around eight taken after listening to the news, 'always dreadful', on Geoff Bostock's wireless, followed by a wash in a tin bath, one for each tent – theirs had a large hole in it – and then to bed.

When they reached Tamu the terrain changed dramatically and the going got much tougher. They were now about to cross mountains five thousand feet high on a track so narrow and precipitous that they could only take half the elephants. It also meant discarding tents, camp beds, bedding, baths, any little extras – leaving only the barest essentials. There was also the ever-present threat of cholera for they were now on one of the main evacuation routes out of Burma. They began to see, 'wretched Indian evacuees… little graves by the road side.' All members of the party had been inoculated against the disease and every one carried their own drinking water, boiled and filtered. There was no spare water for washing of hands or bathing now as it was all needed for the elephants. They fed the children and themselves under mosquito nets and at night slept in unfinished refugee camps, bamboo shelters, on hard little bunks or on the ground.

My mother writes, 'We started at the crack of dawn so as to get the worst over before the heat. We got up at 5am dressed and packed by a wee torch and were off by 6.30 and marched the first few miles in the dark. It was pretty tiring as it was either a fearful up or down hill, one almost as bad as the other. We did six or seven miles a day.'

And yet, though the terrain was tougher than any of them had ever experienced, they were young and fit, and the scenery was magnificent. Reading her descriptions in the letters there's a definite sense of her enjoying this extraordinary experience, as well as a pride in achieving it.

Finally at Palel in Assam, India, after 142 miles through some of the most inhospitable terrain on earth they reached the road head where they left the elephants – a sad parting – and were taken in stages by lorry first to Imphal, capital of Manipur state, then to the rail head at Dimapur, and thence by train to Calcutta.

After my parents parting at Mawlaik at the start of the trek, my father had been put in charge of government evacuation camps on the more northerly Sittang to Tamu route into India. Some 150,000 evacuees were to pass through in the next few months in terrible conditions as the monsoon set in. Eventually as the Japanese approached, the route was closed. He himself walked north through the Naga Hills, eventually, after two months, reaching Kohima in Assam, the scene two years later of some of the fiercest fighting of the war. He was then relocated by the company to Cochin state in Kerala, south west India, to manage the teak forests for the allied war effort. My mother had gone ahead to the old colonial hill station of 'Ootie' (Ootacomund). It was nearly four months before he was able to re-join her in south west India. In all that time she had no word of him. She always said that this was the worst time of all, not knowing whether he was alive or not.

Many of my father's friends had joined up in Burma at the start of the war. On the wall of his office at home I remember he had a photo – it's here in the folder along with the letters – of the pre-war rugby team he had captained in Rangoon: thirteen out of the fifteen young men pictured never survived the war: they were either killed in battle, died in Japanese POW camps or on the Burma railway. He knew that what he did was vital war work but I know he regretted not being able to join them in fighting 'the Japs'. Though things might have been very different for our family if he had.

I've been nearly an hour reading Mum's letters, totally absorbed in these events of long ago. It's as if I've been listening to her tell the story. It's been a lovely meeting. I'm stiff from kneeling on the landing beside the drawer I was carrying.

Reliving their experiences brings home to me – if ever it were necessary – just how small and insignificant are our present woes by contrast to the times they lived in.

*****

There is a call on my mobile: Alastair has arrived at the edge of the village. It is time to hand over Pop. We pack her belongings – her bed, her bowl and her lead – and without too much encouragement she hops into the boat, carefully seating herself in the stern to keep her bottom dry. We gently push her through the flood, up the road to where Alastair and my sister-in-law Kathy are waiting for us at the water's edge. Big hugs and we stow Pop in the back of their car. She knows them well and I can tell she is happy to be getting out. Alastair comes back with us to the house with the waders and a heap of stores for us stranded souls. I see the look of shock on his face as he registers the flood, the devastation in the house that he knows so well.

Soon after he and Kathy have left, a canoe turns into the drive paddled by Roddy and Holly, our good friends from just down the road. We've known them almost as long as we've been in Somerset. Both self-employed: Roddy is a stonemason, Holly a jeweller. They are able to paddle straight into the conservatory and tie up to a table leg. They haven't seen us since the house flooded. Showing them round, I note the shock in their eyes. They are full of sympathy and commiseration. They join us for a lunch of soup and cheese and we sit at the table in the conservatory, our legs resting on chairs in front of us to keep them out of the water. We've already discovered, you can get very cold very quickly, sitting with legs immersed, even in thick neoprene waders. Their house is still dry but they think it will only be a matter of time before the water is in. Conversation is all about flood, rainfall, height of the water, who's flooded and who hasn't, and the total silence and seeming incompetence of the Environment Agency. All of this with heavy lashings of gallows humour which helps raise the spirits.

Flooding does bring some small compensations, we discover: things don't break if you drop them, dregs of drinks, tea or coffee, can be tossed overboard, just as the crumbs can be swept off the table at the end of a meal.

In a strange way, it's been a good day, a lot achieved: the electrics are safe, we have lights, we have hot water and a plug socket, we have a boat and waders, Poppy is safe and apparently already languishing on a sofa at my brother's. But we are exhausted, drained of emotion and in bed by eight o'clock. Surely a world record. Sleep for both of us is broken, full of jagged dreams.

SUNDAY JANUARY 5TH

The water in the hall at the bottom of the stairs is now four inches deep, in the old part it is ten; pretty much they are always six inches apart. I'm beginning to keep a log to record the depths. It's the first thing I do when I get up in the morning. I keep pad and pencil and the tape measure on the window sill nearest to the bottom step. Somehow this process of logging, recording the data helps restore some small measure of order in all the chaos. Makes me feel we're in control, not the other way round. Already the flood seems to have erased all character and warmth from downstairs; surveying it each morning from the bottom step, the house is cold, lifeless and echoes like a sea cave to the slosh of our wellies.

Mysteriously a tiny snail with a whorled shell has taken up residence on the window sill beside the pad and pencil. How did he get there? Another evacuee perhaps.

The staircase that leads upstairs turns at right angles after a few steps and at this point there is a mini–landing which we have designated our landing stage. It's become the new front door to our living quarters like the entrance to an upper floor apartment. Utta has rescued a doormat for our wellies while the new sets of waders from Alastair are draped down the stair rail. Their trailing legs call to mind two drunks sprawled on the stairs. Putting them on is not to be taken lightly, almost as bad as wrestling into a wet suit. Getting them off is even worse and can take even longer. An unexpected bonus is that for the female form they are definitely figure enhancing: Utta looks very shapely in hers. In the meantime we are learning very quickly that everything takes far longer. Gone is that freedom just to dash downstairs to answer a knock at the door or to get something we've forgotten. Each move has to be planned in advance. We even make lists as if going shopping so that once downstairs we can make the most of it, gathering things we might need.

For Sunday lunch we are invited to Evie's at the mill for a curry, nine of us in all comprising the two different tribes: those who have flooded and those who are dry. Here on the first floor above the boom of the river below, it's warm and cosy in the wood-panelled kitchen. Easy to imagine the working mill, sound of the mill race, creak of its timbers; there are still flaps in the ceiling through which the grain sacks were hoisted to the upper floor. The company, the good food, are just what's needed now, restorative escape for a while from our watery cell. By the time we get home, the level has risen another inch.

At lunch at Evie's there is much talk about insurance companies as well as several scare stories from 2012: so-and-so having had to pay some colossal excess and premium after the last flood. None of us who have flooded have yet spoken to our respective companies. And we are all nervous. On Monday morning I take the plunge. First of all there is panic as I can't find the policy; I rummage feverishly through the files where it should be and just when I think it might have floated out of the door, I find it staring at me on the top of my in tray. I have no recollection of putting it there. Even under normal circumstances in our daily life Utta and I lose things all the time: our glasses, the car keys, a book, the dog's lead, gloves; one or other of us always seems to be looking for some item that we will often find while searching for something else. Now, flooded, living in this world of chaos and disorder, the loss rate seems to have rocketed. 'Darling, have you seen my…?' But there's a positive side to this for as we move 'stuff' upstairs there'll come a cry, 'Guess what! You'll never guess what I've found' and something that vanished months ago, long since written off, is uncovered hiding under a pile of books or papers. There is much joy in being reunited with that which was lost. Life has become a sort of mad recycling process: lose one, find one.

The insurance company, when I get through, are helpful and reassuring. Yes, they have our details and we are insured against flooding. Ashamed to say over all these years I'd never even bothered to check. Someone will be in touch. That someone calls back and I give them a brief description of our situation but as I do, I have the strange sensation that I'm describing someone else's plight, not our own. I can't quite connect, it's a sort of denial, I suppose. We decide it's not worth their coming to see us until the water recedes, when the driers will go in and when we can all see the full extent of the damage. In the meantime, we tell them we're not moving, we will stay in the house. It's a relief to have made contact. In the course of conversation I learn that Nick, our neighbour, is insured with the same company so they will visit us both when the time comes.

Our rain gauge has floated away, carried off by the flood but we have a pretty good idea of rainfall by the water that's collected in the bottom of the boat now tethered to the bench outside. What matters is inside, for each day the water level in the house creeps up. Eight inches on Monday, January 6th, nine and a half on Tuesday, up to ten – over the bottom step of the stairs – to twelve inches by Thursday. Eighteen in the old part. At these depths it's well over the top of wellies; any journey downstairs now means changing into waders. Our

beloved house is drowning in front of our eyes. Over the next
few days there is so much to do, shifting stuff from downstairs
to safety upstairs, it helps to keep our minds off the sight of the
house being overwhelmed, its light and warmth snuffed out.
Unrecognisable. It gives us a glimpse of what it must be like
for families caught up in conflicts around the world – far, far
worse for them – but still that same loss of everything familiar.

Gradually though, like Robinson Crusoe on his desert
island, we begin to establish fresh patterns of living to adapt
to this new landscape, to life on the upper deck. From the
one plug in the kitchen we trail power cables for kettle and
appliances, bring up a camping gas burner for quick cooking
to create a sort of breakfast bar outside our room at the end
of the landing so that we can have our early morning cup of
tea in bed, followed by breakfast on the bathroom floor, now
the new kitchen table. Anything to avoid going downstairs
without proper cause and having to put on waders. We've
taken to reading in bed with our tea, a delicious luxury. No
pumps to service, we're off duty now. One morning as Utta
sips her cuppa, admiring the play of dappled light reflected on
the ceiling from the floodwater below,

'Oh, it's so beautiful,' she muses, 'I've always wanted to
live by water.'

How fortunate, I think to myself, to be married to this
person. Talk about making the best of things.

Every day we try to have lunch in the conservatory,
the light is important to us, the house has become so cold
and dark inside. In the evening we have supper sitting on the
bathroom floor, with tablecloth and candlelight. We still cook
the evening meal downstairs in the kitchen on the leaning gas
hob but whoever's chef has to remember everything, otherwise
it means putting the waders back on to fetch the salt or the
mustard or a glass. Or, much more important, the wine.

Food has necessarily become very simple; things that
can be cooked quickly on the gas top: sausages, pasta, liver
and bacon, eggs. And then there are surprising things, long

forgotten, that we find in the freezer. The big one outside in its own shed has had to be abandoned, the power to its socket switched off, but we have rescued some of its contents and transferred them to a smaller freezer that Glen next door has helped me carry out to the garden shed where it sits on blocks at a drunken angle, connected by yet another electrical cable looped across the garden. The shed has also become a refuge for other sheltering migrants, mice and rats in particular. They have created their own entrance, a large hole gnawed through the planking. I am not that keen to meet them. As I approach in my waders, usually in the dark, I make lots of noise and bang on the door. Rummaging in the freezer is like prospecting. I unearth frozen stews that Utta made last year or even before, ancient lamb chops – very tasty still – hot smoked salmon steaks, even the odd pudding and other surprises that I bring inside like the hunter home from the hill, 'Guess what! Look what I found!'

*****

Having lost the use of the floor and with so much furniture taken upstairs there is a desperate shortage of shelf space for plates, bowls, all the kitchen kit accumulated over thirty years. It is hugely satisfying to find just the right piece of wood from the shed in the garden to bridge a gap to provide a new shelf, or to make a coat rack for wet weather kit from a pole over the top of two doors in the conservatory lashed down with gaffer tape. It's basic improvisation, problem-solving of the simplest kind, the sort of thing you do when camping. It's also another of those things, like keeping a record of the flood depth, which helps us feel we're achieving something, taking back control and lifting us out of the gloom and despondancy. It's the fun and satisfaction, too, of seeing a use for things for which they were not actually designed but which work perfectly in their new role, recycling materials. Utta is very good at this.

Meanwhile outside, queues of bobbing apples hang around the doors hoping to be allowed in. Like children waiting to come in out of the rain. We try and repel them by opening the door wide and sweeping them away but when you close it they are sucked back in and sneak round the edge. They always seem terribly excited to have made it inside and set off exploring the rooms tagging along in the wake of our waders. Worst is the green duck weed that gets into everything, along with sticks and clumps of vegetation.

*****

Though we feel we are adapting and finding ways of living in our flooded home, there is one area that we find most difficult. And it's one that all of us who've flooded ask of each other, albeit somewhat surreptitiously, 'What are you doing about going to the loo?' In fact Roddy has already written to the Prime Minister asking him how he'd like to shit in a bin liner on the bathroom floor. To which there has not yet been a reply.

Here at Willow Cottage, as with all our neighbours, the drains are under water, there's nowhere for it to go. Getting rid of our waste, the need to distance ourselves from it is such a primal thing. To discharge water alone is fine, we wash up the few plates and cups we use, our washing we take to kind friends, we have no qualms about letting out the bath, or flushing after a pee – if it adds to the flood water, so be it. But what to do about having a crap, that daily ablution so much part of our lives. There are those who might be able to hold it until they can get out to dry land and a friendly loo up the road, but neither of us are built that way. I'm certainly not.

I was brought up in the 1950s when the schools I attended were imbued with the principles of muscular Christianity, fresh air, shorts in all seasons and above all the need to 'go regular'. In fact going regular seemed so important I was sure it was one of the reasons why we had won the war. At my first small prep school in North Cornwall I was normally a day boy but on one occasion when my parents had to be away for my sister's prize day I was obliged to board for a couple of nights and of course fell under the school's regime. Anxious about the need to perform on cue, I immediately became constipated and failed matron's after-breakfast check at which we were given either a tick or cross on her clipboard list. 'You'll have to come back this afternoon after games,' she said, 'for another go.' I spent the rest of the day in a state of mounting anxiety. Lunch of rabbit on the bone – it must have been a Thursday – with lumpy mashed potato and cabbage certainly didn't help. The rabbit was always badly skinned and it came with quite a lot of fur still attached; you had to push it to one side and hide it under a piece of cabbage. It was on the way back from the playing fields, increasingly sure that I'd never be able to earn my tick, that I happened to spot some fallen twigs on the path under the trees, amongst them a short stubby one about the size of a cork which I quickly pocketed. Later I met matron outside the junior lavatories at the appointed hour and she asked, 'So, have you been?'

'Yes miss.' She strode past and peered down into the cubicle at my wooden replica floating happily in full view. Fortunately she wore glasses and was rather short sighted. 'Good boy,' she purred, and ticking me off her list, was off on her rounds.

So, being regular, Utta and I have decided the best approach is to use a bucket, the lowest one we can find so that we can squat over it easily. It's a solution but there is no pleasure in my early morning ablution, instead I am beginning to dread it. The sight and the smell is awful, a further desecration of our beloved home. Though we spread newspaper under the bucket this performance takes place on the bathroom floor which is also where we have our evening meal. Too close for comfort. The squatting position, doctors tell us, is actually the best, the most natural way to perform, but this is not like being in the wild where a crap with a view of woods and hills – and well buried after – can be a memorable experience; here the bucket, however low, always prevents you from getting right down to relax on your haunches so it's always uncomfortable and a strain on the legs. As self- appointed night soil man, I then change into waders and take the buckets outside, tipping them into the 'solids' part of the cesspit, shortcutting the flooded drains. One morning early I realise I've forgotten to collect Utta's. She calls me from an upstairs window,

'Don't come up, I've had an idea, wait there,' she calls. In a moment her bucket with lid, suspended from two scarves knotted together, is lowered carefully down from above. The term 'supply drop' takes on new meaning. Did Rapunzel do this sort of thing, I wonder.

Our ablutions are so much part of the routine of our normal daily lives, like brushing our teeth, making the first morning cup of tea, we tend not to think of them. It's only when that routine is disrupted as it is now that I'm reminded that some of the most challenging experiences especially when I was young have had to do with loos. Especially in France.

My very first encounter with French plumbing was when, aged fifteen, I spent a fortnight on an exchange visit to a family in Normandy, in a rambling old farmhouse that had seen better days. My room was on the first floor down the landing from the lavatory. I was totally unprepared for the sight that greeted me when I first opened the door: two china footsteps were positioned either side of a drain hole, it was as if the plumber had forgotten to fit a proper pedestal and seat. Once I'd worked out how to proceed I pulled the stiff piece of bent wire that served as a chain and nearly drowned under a deluge of water that swirled around me, threatening to soak my feet. Before this happened however there was another dilemma: there seemed to be no loo paper, only a butcher's hook on the wall with strips of newspaper impaled upon it. So where was the loo paper? I wondered. Looking around there seemed to be nothing else. The newspaper was well within reach, so it was obviously for reading or using, perhaps both. Perhaps it was Monsieur's morning reading. If it was, I worried I might cause a diplomatic incident if I used it. I tore off a strip and could just make out something about de Gaulle and Algeria but the text had been ripped in half. I stood in a quandary, undecided. To wipe or not to wipe? But I'd now been in there so long I was in danger of activating a manhunt. So taking the plunge I used the newsprint. It was very unforgiving, rough as sandpaper, but it worked. By the end of my stay I got quite used to it, rather fond of its scratchy texture. Certainly a lot better than the terrible Bronco we used at home, thin as rice paper and shiny on one side. Only good for tracing paper.

The unexpected bonus to all this was that my room was almost opposite that of the daughter, a lovely young woman in her early twenties, on holiday from her job in Paris. In the mornings she was being fitted for a dress for some special occasion and through the door, open in the warm weather, I could see her surrounded by her mother, a maiden aunt and another friend. It was like a scene out of Degas or one of the Impressionists: the bowed heads, soft murmur of voices, mouths full of pins, a peaceful intimacy as they clucked and pinned the paper patterns around her body. There'd be glorious glimpses of her bare back, shoulder or waist and I'd slow my steps in passing as far as I decently could, inhaling this vision of beauty before reeling off down the corridor.

★★★★★

Over the weekend and at the start of the week reports are coming in thick and fast of the impact and devastation of the flood. Muchelney is now totally cut off, all four roads in and out are impassable. Here on our side of Thorney, Roddy and Holly have now flooded, so too Rita and Chris who live opposite them, even Glen and Sue next door. Their house, built on ground rising sharply to the humpback bridge, was always thought safe, but flood water is nature's spirit level, making connections on the ground never deemed possible. In flood conditions every centimetre counts, the difference between remaining dry – or months of chaos.

In the 'other' Thorney over the bridge, another nine properties have gone under, most of them flooded for the second time after 2012, as have the Nightingales at Muchelney Ham, their flood defences, big diesel pumps, overwhelmed like ours. Since our computer connection is under water we rely heavily on others, usually Roddy, for information about the flood. The EA seems a bit like a department store going bust, there's a lot of window dressing, flashy weather updates and telemetry – the height of the water at various points around the moor, but there doesn't seem to be a lot going on inside. Letting us know the height of the river is one thing, telling us how they plan to prevent it flooding our homes is another. Even their telemetry seems confused: at one point Roddy is phoned by one of their automatic alerts where a voice informs him the threat of flood has passed. This might have been reassuring were it not for the fact that as he answers the phone he is already standing in three inches of water.

It is late afternoon on Sunday. I walk down river toward the pumping station. The water now so high that the bank is just a thin divide; to one side the moor like a wild sea, brown-grey churned by the wind, great logs and pieces of timber, dead wood dashed onto the shore of the bank, while on the other side the river slides by, huge and dark, eddies coiling and uncoiling. In the corner of one field, hemmed in by the fence, a great mat of brown reed and debris has collected around a dead bullock, half submerged, already a hole in its side punctured by foxes and crows the better to rummage inside it. The sky is dark, menacing. Heavy with rain to come. It's hard to reconcile this grim, angry landscape with the peace and tranquillity of the moor we have come to know so well. It's like seeing someone you've loved and trusted all your life acting in an unrecognisable and ugly manner. You feel betrayed. Let down.

And then a wild ululation in the sky: a flock of geese straining against the wind, urging each other on with their wild cries. Good or bad omen, I don't care, they lift the spirits.

Chapter Five

GETTING OUT

Monday January 6th

The tractor run is now in full swing. It's the week after the Christmas break, work starting again. We are very lucky here to have farmers and others who know exactly what to do in times like these, quickly providing, without being asked, a remarkably efficient and reliable service through the floods. Voluntarily and at entirely their own cost. The tractor belongs to Mike Curtis, who farms on the northern side of Thorney, the other side of the river from us. The trailer has been loaned by the forge, metal fabricators on the old milk marketing board site. The main driver is Mike's father-in-law, Richard England. They've done this before – and not so long ago in 2012 – there's a well-rehearsed routine. And it's relentless. Pick up in Thorney, their side of the river for the 7.30 and 8.30 morning run, regular as a clock. Drop off down the road where the cars are parked. More runs throughout the day. Back again in the evening to collect those returning after a day's work around five and six o'clock.

It's only a short stretch up the flooded road past our house – about 150 yards – but a vital one, impossible to get through otherwise without waders or boat and certainly not with children. From our upstairs window, like an observation platform or the deck of a ship, we can see them pass: often a wave from Richard, his passengers seated on bales in the back or standing, holding onto the gate of the trailer at the front. In the mornings they tend to sit, often hunched against the cold or wet, not talking, not fully awake. In the evenings it's different, especially on a dry night; like a plane landing, there's even a ladder to help them down, laughter and buzz and chat, passengers spilling off and smiling faces, some clutching shopping and bags, happy to be back. All journeys now start and end at this flooded road, a good metre deep. In some ways it is our river Styx of Greek myth that separated the world of the living from the world of the dead. It's the great divide, our prison gate. Beyond is the outer world, ordinary daily life. This side, locked in by the flood, normal life has floated away. This side is disorder, chaos, constraint.

But things are not all bad and life goes on. On the first Monday of the week as I'm setting off for a walk down the river bank, the afternoon tractor returns and amongst the passengers getting off are a young couple, Kate and Nigel Bunce. Nigel is a thatcher, a very good one. With their one little boy, they live almost opposite John Leach's pottery; they too have been flooded and for the second year running. Seeing their happy faces, catching their excitement as we greet each other, I'm surprised that they're not more sombre, fed up with what life has thrown at them.

'Have you just been shopping?' I ask.

'Well we have, but the reason we went into Yeovil was the hospital appointment', Kate is bursting to tell the good news, 'We're going to have another baby!' And then adds,

'If it's a boy, we think we might call him Noah!'

★★★★★

For those of us living on the flooded road, there is no point in taking the tractor, it's only a short distance to dry land. We all use waders but we each have other means of getting out

depending on circumstances. Glen and Sue next door have a
very stable Indian canoe. Glen is a cabinet maker, currently
working in the next village and loads the canoe with his tools
and gear needed for the kitchen he is installing. Resourcefully
he balances whole pre-made sections on cross supports before
gently paddling down the road where he'll transfer them to
his vehicle. The far end of the flood has turned into a sort of
small dock, a shipping quay for loading and unloading cargo.
It's grubby and scuffed by vehicles turning. Replacing the tang
of the sea is even the dank smell of the flood from the clumps
of grass and weed washed up from the moor. Cars have parked
as close to the water as they safely can so the owners, reaching
dry land, can make a quick get-away. These slots have become
premium parking. Much sought-after. We are very spoilt as
Niall Christie who lives just beyond the reach of the water has
given us our own parking space outside his house.

WEDNESDAY JANUARY 8TH

*7.30am. Water depth, eleven and a half inches at the bottom
of the stairs, seventeen and a half in the old part. Think it's
slowing. River is down, below the level at which it will spill
over further down. Which will help.*

*Candlelit supper last night on the bathroom floor. Baked
beans and chorizo followed by lemon pud that I found in
the freezer in the shed. Very old but very tasty! Much
phoning; Emily and Oliver checking in, may see them at
Ali and Kathy's. Didn't sleep well. OK till 3-ish then lying
awake, mind churning. Up at 6.45. Back exercises. Bucket
dump. Tea for two. Muesli in bed and read, Merivel by
Rose Tremain. One of her best. I'm lost in it. Wonderful.
Clear morning, reflected light on ceiling. Into waders, work
in kitchen, making space. Each time go down, like entering
Hades. Dark soup of duckweed, sticks and apples bobbing.
Like a bad dream. So incongruous. Is this real? Has it really
happened to us? Such a violation. It's that that shocks.*

If we're going anywhere by car, shopping or to see friends – often with washing – we take our boat. Yet packing and preparing for such a short journey can be long and complicated. We could be off to France for all the kit that's involved. We change into waders on the landing then, clutching clothes and shoes needed for the other side, wet weather gear in case, all the bits required for shopping, the bundle of washing we're going to drop in at friends along the way, we wade through the house to the conservatory to where the boat is tied up outside, gently swivelling on its rope in the wind. Half full of water from the rain in the night, it takes several minutes to bail out. I then realise I've left my mobile phone, my only means of communication, in the bathroom upstairs. As I'm going back inside anyway, Utta adds a small extra shopping list of her own of things she hasn't exactly forgotten but it would be good to have with her anyway. So it's back to the half landing, change out of waders, collect phone, items on her list, reboot and re-descend. At last ready to go, Utta climbs aboard steadying our various bags while I wade behind gently propelling her and the boat across the flooded lawn and up the road. At the far end we pull up on the grass beyond the 'Anchorage' belonging to Chris and Rita, the last of the flooded houses. The car is only yards away. It's beginning to rain again.

'Have you got the keys?'

'No, I thought you had them.'

I wade back to find I've left them on the conservatory table. And we're off at last. From start to finish this small operation has probably taken the best part of an hour. Just to get to the car.

Today we're going into Langport, a journey that normally takes little more than five minutes but with the Muchelney road flooded now means a half an hour detour. We are retired, for us this is merely an inconvenience. The town is grey, battened down, the river Parrett huge, like a great brown python coiling under the bridge, nearly up to the arches. Many of the buildings on the Westover Trading Estate

on the other side of the river have flooded or are threatened by
flood water. But the town side is still dry, the hairdresser tells
me as I have my hair cut. The salon is small and functional, a
warm cocoon. Two elderly ladies are having their hair done,
their intimate chat and murmured conversations each with
their hairdresser has something of the confessional. Carol who
cuts my hair is well informed through her customers about the
local area and which roads are still clear; through the media she
knows Muchelney is cut off. What is interesting and perhaps
a measure of the focus on Muchelney is that she has no idea of
the flooding in Thorney and beyond. It's as if we do not exist.

The gentle atmosphere of the salon is in stark contrast to
having my hair cut as a child in the holidays in my home town
of Okehampton in Devon where we moved after Cornwall.
Dad would drop my brother and I off at the tobacconists which
gave through to the barber's shop, a tiny battered room like
a cave, set round with hard wooden chairs and men waiting,
full of fug and fag smoke, thick with gossip and raincoats – it
always rained in 'Okey'. Here we received the standard 'short
back and sides' from an ex-Army barber, quick as a shearer,
who only paused to exchange football scores and comment on
local news. At the end, squeezing the bulb of a large brown
spray bottle he'd shower us with 'bay rum,' a sweet sickly-
smelling liquid like a drench. It was 'one and six and pay on
the way out'. We'd emerge practically shaven, bald as monks,
just a small patch of hair on top.

Hairdressing completed, we do something we've only
done very rarely: we buy fish and chips for lunch and as it's
still raining, eat them in the car. Like OAPS, which we are,
but pretend not to be. We then move to the coffee shop nearby
and voraciously read the papers which we haven't seen for over
a week.

Langport is not at its best in the slanting rain, grey and
deserted. Yet this small town, where the houses in the street
leading down to the river lean gently backward like tired old
men, was once a vibrant trading hub, with thriving cattle

market, two stations and a colourful, watery history. Here the river is hemmed in by a ridge of low hills, the ancient cliff line, before flowing across the flat Sedge Moor to Bridgwater and the coast. For hundreds of years, the river was the main highway from the port of Bridgwater and the coast 14 miles away right up until the coming of the railways in the 1850s. Long, narrow, flat-bottomed barges, up to 50ft long, made use of the high tides and tidal bore to propel them up-river to Stanmoor above Burroughbridge, carrying twenty to thirty tons of coal or brick and stone from Bridgwater, returning with agricultural produce. From Stanmoor, horses were used to complete the last six miles or so to Langport. The journey could be done in a day. Most barges had a crew of two men, a captain and mate. Many of them came from boating families, starting young and spending a lifetime on the river. The main shippers in the business were the Stuckey and Bagehot company with a fleet of at least fifty vessels. In its heyday some 60-70,000 tons of traffic was moved by river each year bringing employment and prosperity to Langport. To ease the journey, cider houses grew up along the way. At the head of the tidal reach Langport prospered, a distribution centre and entrepot for transport of goods onward by river and canal; it was said that there were sea captains aplenty along the river and by the wharves.

So close to the river the town was always vulnerable to flooding. In the early 1890s floodwater reached the level of the upper windows in the lower town. Minor floods occurred regularly but one of the biggest came in the October of 1960 when the town was seriously threatened as were the whole of the Levels and surrounding areas. The papers were full of graphic reports of flooded streets in Taunton, banks giving way up and down the Parrett, closure of many roads and increasing fears for the residents of Langport. It became national news, the situation even debated in Parliament. Grand schemes of flood prevention were discussed by government and County Council.

On the night of 27th October 1960 as the flooding worsened around Langport a local councillor, Hugh Binder, suggested bringing back into operation an old pump, an 8-inch Invincible made by the famous British engineering company J&H Gwynne. It had served the town well over several decades to pump away flood water within the town's flood banks as well as getting rid of escaped sewage from the rhyne encircling part of the town. Binder approached a young engineer, Chris Osborne, who was at the time working on the installation of a new sewage system for the town, and who tells the story,

'I was in me wellies because the water was up to me shins and I was working in the workshop when this chap called Hugh Binder walked in. He said, 'Chris, this bloody flood is getting serious.'

Binder told him about the pump and Osborne agreed to have a go at getting it to work again. They found it in the bushes by the rhyne. Derelict, it hadn't been used in years.

'We pulled en out with a tractor. He was all rusted up, wouldn't move. So we got en back to the workshop and I started to take en apart. The bolts round the pump casing were all rusted in, had to give it a good tap and then use the biggest set of stilsons I had to shift them, then I worked on easing the impellor, replaced the glands and bearings, packed in a lot of grease, totally cleaned it up.' He worked day and night to restore it.

Some half a dozen Green Goddess army fire engines were already pumping but making little impression on the rising waters. By 3.15am the following night, the pump was ready. It was belt-driven so a Fordson Major tractor had been brought in from High Ham to power it. Once it was connected up and running the pump, Osborne says 'it worked like a dream, a remarkable piece of engineering. It pulled off one inch of water in the first hour.'

They got hold of a second pump, an American BUDA, diesel-driven. Chris remembers it came with the slogan, 'Unsurpassed for Pumping Fast, and made in the USA.'

Together in the next hour the two pumps together pulled off another two inches of water.

They knew then that Langport could be saved. The old pump has been restored and sits in its own space behind the old town hall; as the plaque says, 'a vital part of the town's history and heritage'. The story of the pump is also a measure of the resourcefulness, skill and sheer determination of men like Osborne and his mates who worked 36 hours without sleep to get it going – Chris eventually fell asleep on his work bench with his head propped on the vice.

★★★★★

To round off our day out we are invited to supper with our good friend, Jane Lang, in Curry Rivel, near Langport. It was with Jane and her husband Anthony that I stayed in their welcoming farmhouse when I first came to Somerset to go elvering in the early 1970s. It was on their farm that the elver-holding tanks were sited. Jane, now on her own, still very good looking, is an excellent cook and gives us delicious roast belly of pork, roast potatoes and vegetables, all beautifully cooked. Conversation is always easy with Jane, she is interesting and interested, with a natural curiosity. She asks questions, always relevant, 'Now tell me about…' On her i-pad she shows us pictures of her grandchildren. We agree on the way home that if we can be a fraction as mentally active when we are her age, we will be happy.

Returning home we find someone has taken our slot and we have to park further up the road. It's everything in reverse now, changing back into waders, gathering bags and bundles, shopping, piles of post, finding somewhere dry to put them down while we right the upturned boat. It has started to rain again. The flooded road eerily quiet as I wade along pushing the boat with Utta on board holding the bundles. Standing in the dark outside the house we search for the key.

I realise I've left it in the car. I wade back to fetch it. When I return, Utta is tight-lipped, steely. Announces she's going to stay in bed next day. Fortunately, next morning, 'sleep that knits the ravelled sleave of care' has helped her forget – Utta always sleeps like a log – and she wakes perky as a lark and revived by her early morning cuppa bought to her by her butler and night soil man.

★★★★★

Today's task is moving books upstairs. Suspended above the flood, we realise they are beginning to get damp, the pages absorbing the moisture, just beginning to swell. Taking them off the shelves, packing them into boxes or simply making piles on the half way landing to be carried up later is like meeting old friends from the past. They come in all shapes and sizes, some still unread, some forgotten, some vividly remembered for their language or humour or slant on life. They've all been important. We are what we read: they bring back memories not just of what they were about, but how we acquired them; sometimes where and when I read them. I think to myself,

'Yes, I remember you, I remember reading you half the night during a break in the elver fishing on the Laxford in Scotland, that must have been years ago, when the children were still little. But such a good read. I couldn't put you down. Thank you so much for that. No, I couldn't possibly throw you away. Don't worry, you're safe. I'm keeping you.'

Sometimes I remember where I read them because of the sheer contrast, the incongruity between the landscape of the book and where I happened to be at the time: the leafy green parks and country houses of Jane Austen enjoyed years ago on a searing hot beach in Crete or the world of George Elliot's Middlemarch devoured in the mountains of the Hindu Kush. Perhaps they made even more of an impression because of that contrast. All these books have given such pleasure, transported me to another world.

My father used to read a great deal, easily a book a week. He was well-known at our local library. When he retired and came home from abroad, he would read after lunch, tucked into a book in his armchair, and later as he grew older, he would put the book aside and settle himself for 'forty winks'. Now also retired, I try and do the same, though always torn between the need to read the paper and the wish to read the book. And I can nod too. I can always tell if it's a good read because I don't nod as much and I am suddenly aware it's three o clock and I should be weeding or mowing or attending to some vital household chore. But it was my grandmother who inspired the idea of writing down the books you read. She was of the generation that got her books from the Harrods Lending Library; they came in neat bundles, four or five books, in a canvas sling held firm by straps. When she'd read them, she simply wrapped them up and sent them back. To prevent herself from reordering a book she'd already read, she kept a record of the title and the author in a little notebook.

'What are these ticks for, Gran?' I remember asking her, when she showed me the notebook.

'Oh, those are if I've enjoyed it.'

'This one's got four ticks.'

'Oh yes, that was a lovely book. I shall probably ask for it again.' She was a great Jane Austin fan and returned to her again and again. She loved the dialogue which she found amusing and made her chortle. So I too now have a reading log, started in 1972. I find it has become almost a diary, a reminder of what I was reading and when, vital as reference for titles and authors whose names I've forgotten – increasingly used for this purpose. Though I always have a book on the go, over forty years of reading occupies pathetically little space in my logbook; all that pleasure given, those insights into this rich and infinitely varied world, all reduced down into these few thin pages. In a way it's like a summary of one's life, an obituary.

★★★★★

Meanwhile upstairs in the two bedrooms which we have made our temporary holding-store, it is becoming difficult to move. There's been no time to sift and sort and stack in orderly piles, instead it's more like layers of sediment deposited, the first things to be brought up lying at the bottom. Piles of books teeter on top of kitchen plates on top of rugs, cushions and carpets; pictures are piled on boxes of cutlery and cups, whole drawers pulled from desks still full of contents scatter the beds, clothes piled on top. It is one huge jumble and it will all need sorting but at least it is out of the flood. In many ways it represents the chaos that has invaded our lives at the moment. Yet we find, as the days pass, that any little thing we do to improve our situation, small achievements – putting up a temporary shelf, setting up chairs by the window in our bedroom where can read – are a huge boost to morale. Like a gleam of sun.

FRIDAY JANUARY 10TH

Water level in main house down one inch to ten and three quarters. A good day, coiling up pipes outside, carrying more books upstairs. A walk to the pumping station. River down but flood still all around. People in much better mood, coping after the shock. Most of us deciding to stay in our homes. Rod and Hol canoe over, tie up to table in conservatory where we have coffee and Viennese swirls from the food hamper that they'd picked up for us. Donated by one of the supermarkets. A tonic to see them.

At the end of the day we pack to leave for the weekend. We are going to stay with my brother Alastair and his wife Kathy in Wiltshire. Emily and Oliver and the grandchildren will all join us there. And we'll see Pop. We are excited by the prospect of getting out, yet there's a hidden anxiety, a reluctance about letting go, leaving the house undefended, vulnerable in the event of another storm and rising water levels. But we know it'll do us good to get out, especially to see the family. And we're getting better at embarkation. Containers are the answer: plastic bins and tubs to put bags of clothing in to keep them dry. However much you bail out, the bottom of the boat is always wet. We leave the boat pegged to the bank at the far end of the village.

On arrival we are given a great welcome, like combatants returning from the front. Poppy, whom Alastair and Kathy have been caring for, is also very pleased to see us. There is much groaning and chest grunting, signs of deep pleasure, her tail working so hard she can barely stand until remembering she hasn't got a present for us she hunts for something suitable – a feather she finds on the drive. With some ostentation she takes us through to the sitting room where she seems to have acquired a large sofa which she has made her own personal bed; I detect a faint hint of 'Much more comfortable than anything we've got a home'. I make a mental note not to worry in any way about her future wellbeing or comfort.

It is only later over tea and good chats in the kitchen that we realise how tired and stressed we have both become. I can feel myself relaxing, muscles un-tensing, mind letting go. Warm and dry and fed and spoiled. It's as if we've been holding a great weight that we now feel able to put down. Yet I still sleep badly. Dreams I can't remember; my mind like an earthworm processing the dark and awful memory of the flood, aerating it, turning it into good soil. Utta on the other hand sleeps like a log and I envy her deep rhythmic breathing as I lie awake.

Our children and grandchildren join us on the Saturday, it is wonderful to be all together. They are avid to know all the news, the details, what it has been like, how high the water, who else affected, above all how the house is. It means a lot to them, they love Willow Cottage and though neither was born there, Oliver was only two and Emily just five when we moved in, it's been their home, their anchorage too, source of all their childhood memories. I'm also aware of something else happening, probably for the first time: in the past through their lives it has been we as parents who have comforted them; now we are aware of their concern and sympathy turned on us and we draw strength from it. Imperceptibly the roles are changing.

Having the grandchildren with us, the three little boys, prevents any descent into emotion or retrospection. I never knew that being a grandparent would be quite so absorbing, so enriching nor that we'd love them with such a fierce intensity. And be able to hand them back. There is an immediacy about them. Totally absorbed in what they are doing, in the games or toys that Kathy brings down from the top of the house. The following morning, at a very early hour, Emily, sharing their room, overhears the conversation between the six year old and his younger brother,

'Ethan, is my nappy dry?' There is the sound of checking, patting.

'Yes, it's dry.'

'I'll probably get a star.'

'I might get a star too. I didn't cry all day yesterday.'

After an evening out or a weekend away the worst part is getting back. For a while it's been possible to forget, suspend reality. Returning comes as a shock. Before the flood, for all these years, coming home has been a welcome ritual after journeys long or short, feeling the house embrace and enfold you. Like a return to harbour followed by the ritual of opening up, greeted by dog or cat, collecting the post from the box, inspecting the veg patch after longer absence, checking messages. Not now. The house is dead, just a shell. Like someone with some terminal illness or dementia, the outline recognisable but all personality, all spirit gone. The water has gone down, but somehow this has made things worse not better, enhancing its ugliness and desolation. Bare walls, mats of rotting apples, duck weed beginning to stink.

Outside the loop, outside the flood, people go about their lives in happy ignorance. Stopping on our way back to pick up milk at the community shop in Kingsbury, a mile down the road, we are asked,

'Were you flooded then?'

'Oh, very sorry to hear about that. Well, expect you're all dried out now.'

Our lives are so cellular, so self-contained; wrapped in my own little life, I would probably have made exactly the same comments. Perhaps it was what Bruegel was saying in his painting of Icarus, who flew too near the sun, melting the wax on his wings. He is depicted falling from the sky, drowning in the sea while the ploughman, shepherd and fishermen go about their daily work unseeing, oblivious to his plight and to the drama in a corner of the picture. I feel we have a certain shared bond with Icarus, not with the flying bit, but with his watery ending, his drowning.

★★★★★

Standing to chat in waders in the flooded road, water up to our waists, has become part of daily life now. I have some of the best chats, intense or hilarious, with people as we pass one another on our way in or out of the village. Quite often I've never met them before but there's a new openness now. And it is because for many of us there is time, time to stop, normal life on hold. At the moment conversation tends to revolve around flood-related matters, water levels, how we're coping, insurance companies. And builders. When it comes to builders, I feel a quickening of the pulse, a growing panic and urgency to get hold of one before they're all booked. Whilst there's nothing they can actually do until the flood recedes and we dry out, at least to have a builder ready to come in would be very reassuring. I can sense a bit of a scrabble, some sharp elbowing in the offing to get one of the recommended ones. It would be awful to have to wait for months. Roddy has already secured a firm in Somerton. Some insurance companies strongly suggest their own building firms but we've been advised against this by Liz and Peter Nightingale based on their marathon experience last year. I phone Richard Lang, at Bowdens Farm near Hambridge, our landlord from our smokery days. Without hesitation he recommends a builder in

Curry Rivel. I take the contact numbers and get in touch. He's in London working on a friend's property but by the time that's finished, he says, the timing might just be right. We agree to stay in touch and keep him up to date with our situation. I feel a deep sense of relief that we have something planned for the rebuilding of our home, for a return to normal life. Something to pin our hopes to.

MONDAY JANUARY 13TH

Remarkable in this little community how quickly the spirit of self-help has arisen: people have begun to assume roles to reconnect the threads of normal life otherwise lost in the flood. The tractor run was the first example of this. Now Rita, who is still flooded but on the edge of the flood water, has taken on the role of postmistress and depot for incoming mail and parcels. We wade up to her house, the Anchorage; the drive and the back are dry but you step down into a flooded kitchen. Two huge dogs the size of cattle share this small space; with husband Chris, they are all now living in two rooms above, together with all their belongings saved from below. She bellows at the dogs who retreat grumbling upstairs. Rita is like some beautiful exotic flower, a colourful mix of Italian parents and London upbringing, warm and friendly and as kind and generous as they come. She works from home arranging overseas conferences; highly organised, she has the post sorted and racked by household.

Dropping in to collect our post calls to mind the old 'poste restante' system as it used to be that enabled travellers to collect their mail from post offices all over the world. It was not unusual to be out of touch for weeks at a time and no one worried, as daily connection by mobile phone and wi-fi just didn't exist back then. I remember the excitement of picking up fat bundles of letters in Ankara, Teheran, Kabul, letters from home, letters from friends that gave hours of delicious reading. Starved for news I'd read and re-read them, squeezing out every drop of information, every nuance – especially if the writer was young and female. And this in turn would lead to hours of response, scrawled on skinny sheets of paper in chai houses or hostels – traveller's tales.

Sometimes no poste restante existed. One winter working for UNICEF as a volunteer in northern Afghanistan in the early 1970s, up in the Wakhan corridor bordered by Russia, China and Pakistan, I met an Afghan postman. A lean, wiry figure, wrapped against the cold, fur hatted, the mail carried in his big leather satchel, well buckled, slung across his shoulder. His face was weathered and creased by the wind but his eyes shone. He radiated energy. He didn't walk, he loped, moving fast and fluid as a wolf, up to thirty miles a day through the mountains where once the Silk Route ran. And where one night in the lights of the jeep a snow leopard bounded across our path.

Here, today, it's the usual faceless bundle of bank statements, bills and drizzle of junk mail. The art of letter writing, of talking to someone on paper, seems to have quietly slipped into oblivion. As I grew up, letter writing was something that became embedded at school, the obligatory letter home to parents, the pencil chewed for inspiration, mostly sporting results,

'Yesterday we played St Petrocs. They won 14-1.'

We were never any good at football and lost by margins so great they could be confused with cricket scores. In reply my parents wrote every week. Mum's letters were always full of descriptions of the garden, 'the daffies are out down in the orchard, wish you could see them, they're a perfect sight' and always ending with health warnings, 'don't forget your scarf to wrap up warm, darling, this wind is bitter, and remember to take your lozenges', these were tiny foul black pills tasting of tar, so strong they puckered the mouth. I had a deep suspicion they were used in road tarmac. My father was the only Dad in the school who wrote letters. His were short and to the point: both sides of one page, and if there was more to say, the sentences spiralled round the margins to the final sign off. All in minute hand, written with energy and at speed. They took a great deal of interpretation and often involved a decipher team of various members of staff who enjoyed puzzling over them, reading bits out loud, hesitating as they worked out the tangled scrawl. By the end practically the whole school would have gathered round to listen and catch up on my family news.

'Bad luck about the dog, Brown. Poor old thing.'

For Utta, writing letters home to Australia to family or friends was a special ritual. Getting home from work after night duty, she'd often sit at the kitchen table in Willow Cottage, a cup of tea beside her. I'd find her immersed in the act of writing, a half smile on her face, either from the telling of some episode or the imagining of that far away land of sunlight, bird sounds and the scent of possibilities.

★★★★★

That night I wade back up to Tony Roberts who lives across from Rita and Chris. He's offered us his gas heater to keep us warm upstairs; heating is the one thing we don't yet have and at night the cold creeps upstairs past the floodwater. Tony's house is built on a rise well above any flood. He is ex-Navy. An engineer by training. A kind and generous man. When we first came to the village we'd take elderly pieces of furniture that he'd skilfully repair for some minute charge. Since the flood he has taken on the role of depot for newspapers and larger items, a role he is enjoying, he tells me as he ushers me in, because it brings people and chat and contact with the community. He is over eighty, living on his own now since his wife died some years ago; winter is a long haul. With age his is shrinking, like us all, but his naval beard and bushy eyebrows remain as jaunty as ever.

As a child in Devon, he recounts proudly, he learned to work with shire horses, to harness and plough with them. Hearing this makes me think that often we don't ask enough of young people, not giving them responsibility by which they can grow and gain confidence. Somehow from horses and childhood, we get onto his time in the Navy and serving in the Far East, just after the war, visiting Nagasaki where you could still see the dark outline on walls of figures atomised by the blast of the bomb. I trundle the heater down to the waiting boat and paddle home through the dark, head still full of those terrible images.

Supper that night on the bathroom floor – with heating. No more sleeping bags. We've entered a new era of comfort.

The next morning, a call from outside. From upstairs, I make out the tall figure of Simon Taylor, straight as a post, clad in voluminous waders, camera slung over shoulder. He and his wife Jayne live on the road to Kingsbury about half a mile beyond the flood. For a while now he's begun to drop by to see if there's anything we want, or need doing, washing, or the use of a shower. Simon is a retired senior police officer. And a lay-preacher. But you'd never know; these facts we've only discovered by degree in conversation. A genuinely kind and caring person and a good listener, eyes twinkling behind glasses, he has the gift of being able to establish a rapport with anyone. He's the ideal look-out and observer, unobtrusively keeping an eye on all of us who've flooded. If he had a crook he'd make a good shepherd.

Over coffee in the conservatory, our legs thrust out on stools, we tell him how angry and let down we feel, letting off steam about the lack of response from the EA and the emergency services, the sense of being utterly forgotten. We reflect on how lucky that this is only a flood not some terrifying nuclear incident at the Hinkley Point Power Station. What then? He nods and listens. We have met Simon several times socially but other than that there has never been the opportunity in our busy lives to do much more than hail each other in passing, often on our bikes. So it is a delight to have time really to chat. This is undeniably one of positives about the flood, about normal busy life being stopped in its tracks. There is time. Time to talk and to listen.

There are other positives too we discover. As our living space is reduced to upstairs, there is no gardening, none of the endless outside jobs, for it's all under water. It's as if we have prematurely moved to smaller accommodation – downsized. Cooking is very basic. Housekeeping and cleaning irrelevant. The computer is dead, the phone doesn't work. We find we have afternoons free. Again there is time. Time to read and reflect. It's a bit like being on the deck of an ancient cruise liner: after lunch we take to sitting in the bedroom by the window on two chairs which up to now have been ornamental, never used. We read wrapped in rugs and watch the light outside. Utta catches my eye, 'I could get used to this!'

'Cuppa tea?'

TUESDAY JANUARY 14TH

The water level in the main house down to three and half inches. Definitely dropping. As a result I see Graham and Helen Walker for the first time. Normally in past floods, Graham, who farms on the edge of Muchelney, a mile down the road from us, has used his tractor and trailer to bring villagers through to Thorney but all this last week the water has been too deep for him. However, this morning early he passes in the tractor, no trailer, just the box on the back. They've been up to collect hay; Helen is lying across the back on the bales, snuggled down. We wave. A delicious peaceful interlude for her.

All roads into Muchelney are submerged. The road to Langport over a mile long, the main artery, is particularly deep. Four feet and more in places. There's an abandoned car, half way along, its roof and aerial just visible, this has become the common marker, depth gauge.

'Oh, water's up again today, just that much of the aerial showing.'

The road to Drayton is much shorter but also very deep and exposed. Muchelney is truly cut off, marooned on its island. To the outside world this is rather quaint, romantic, the notion of an island in the 21st century, a village returned to its original state with its ancient church and abbey. It's been in the headlines before and now the story is dusted off again, reprocessed, and all last week it's been figuring large on the national news, TV, radio and Press, the perfect picture story. Actually for those living there, needing to get to work and the children to school, it is a nightmare. There is also a curious symmetry in the predicament of our two neighbouring communities, just a mile apart, the one actually flooded, the other surrounded by flood. We in Thorney can get out relatively easily; our preoccupation is living in our flooded homes. In Muchelney on the other hand most houses are dry; their preoccupation is transport: getting out – and back again – is a long, laborious business.

That they can get out at all is much due to Alastair Mullineux who lives in the village, a retired chartered surveyor, chairman of the parish meeting. A natural leader and organiser. From the previous flood of 2012 when Muchelney was cut off for some three weeks he learned a lot. Through his contacts in the sailing world, the village was given a rib and outboard which took six to eight passengers and which Alastair ran, three to four trips a day through the flood to Langport. But it lacked power especially in windy conditions. In addition the Burnham-on-Sea Rescue team also generously came down to help; their boat was useful but too small for the numbers involved.

From that experience in 2012 and with twenty children now in the village attending seven different schools, as well as all those going to work, it is time for a more reliable service. What is particularly worrying is that during the first week of being cut off, those desperate to get to work have started to wade using the Drayton road. Mean depth four feet. Just OK in waders in good weather but wait for a westerly and waves chopping the surface, coming home at night, and you're in trouble, deep trouble. Sooner or later someone might drown.

As Alastair says, 'Things have changed so much over the last fifteen or twenty years. Back then if you couldn't get to work, it didn't matter so much, employers more understanding. Now there's so much more pressure not to miss a day.'

It's this fear of possible disaster that he manages to convey forcefully to the council who are jump-started into hiring a boat. It comes from the Wheelie Boat Trust. It's bigger than anything that's been used before, takes 8-10 passengers and designed for the disabled with drop-down bows like a D-Day landing craft. It's arranged that it will be run by Fire and Rescue crews, volunteers mainly from Exmouth. This is its first week in operation and it's already settled into a routine. The first boat leaves at 8am to Langport, and will ply back and forth until the last boat back at 3.45. Cars have already been trailered out down the Thorney road and driven round to a car park close to the flood outside Langport. At the end of the day the boat is then towed back to Exmouth – 50 miles away – for safe keeping in secure overnight storage. The next volunteer crew, working on their days off, must get up at 4am to be back in Muchelney for the morning run. It is relentless. Exhausting. But they are a brilliant team and there's a waiting list for those wanting to do it. The boat is booked for two weeks.

It will be in use for ten.

After the previous flood, Alastair recognised the need for better communication, to be able to let people know on-line when and where the boat was leaving and to post other information affecting the whole community. With the help of Carolyn Roche, village agent for this area, a register of names and contacts was set up. It would probably never be needed, they thought, but useful just in case. Far sooner than anyone imagined, it has become vital.

There are however those on early or late shifts, outside the working hours of the boat, who still have to make their own arrangements to get to work. Gavin Miller from the village is one. Getting up at four in the morning, he is wading through the flood in the dark to reach his car parked on the

Drayton road in order to drive to Bridgwater to start work at six. 'It wasn't frightening,' he says looking back on it, 'I'm used to waders from fly fishing. Beautiful too, out there in the night especially if there was a moon.' I am full of admiration for him. To me it sounds well beyond the call of duty; I never asked him but I hoped that his work recognised his extraordinary sense of duty in making the daily trek.

WEDNESDAY JANUARY 15TH

I sense the fog is beginning to lift. Thorney is being discovered.

A call from James Crowden to see how we're getting on. We've known James for many years. A man of many parts, he's been a soldier, explorer, shepherd, cider maker but is now firmly established as a poet, writer and broadcaster. James would like to bring Martin Hesp, lead writer of the *Western Morning News*, to see us and to show him what things are like here in Thorney.

I meet them at the far end of the flood and load them into the boat. At that precise moment Roddy appears at his front gate as if on cue and when introduced to Martin delivers a fluent, concise synopsis of the flood situation whilst standing in a foot of water. So impressive is it that I'm almost surprised Martin doesn't ask to turn round and go home, having got all he needs. We have lunch in the conservatory – legs propped up as usual. James has brought very good pies to add to the stores. We've asked Liz and Peter Nightingale so Martin can hear their story too. It's good to catch up with them. Utta has a real flair for conjuring things up, giving something simple a sense of ceremony. We have soup, cheese and the pies with a glass or two of wine. It's very relaxed and good to share the grim stories of the flood, laugh about them. Exorcise them.

The next day the flooding of Thorney is the leader page. Thanks to Martin we're on the map. Discovered. The EA will be frantically checking to see where we are.

Today, Friday, another visit. This time Barry James

from Somerset County Council, introduced to us by Carolyn Roche. She and Mike Curtiss had heard he was coming to Muchelney and decided to go down and meet him. The council's understanding had been that as the village had the use of the Wheelie boat, all was well in the area. They met him and suggested he came and saw a place called Thorney up the road. It meant going by tractor. At which he was a little startled. Then further astonished when he learned that the tractor was Mike's. As they progressed he was amazed how bad the flooding was. He visited two or three homes before coming to our side of Thorney, which is when I show him round Willow Cottage. I am impressed, he's not here for show but genuinely concerned by the extent of the flooding, keen to know what has happened. And he listens. He will report back. Things may start to happen.

SUNDAY JANUARY 19TH

Earlier in the week Simon mentioned the possibility of a visit from the bishop of Taunton, keen to see at first-hand how people have been affected by the flood. He arrives with Bishop Peter and the arch-deacon on the back of a tractor, stopping at the edge of the flood where we transfer them into our boat, seating them side by side on the thwart seat. Wading behind pushing the stern gently through the flood, I can hear myself prattling like a tour guide, 'Here on the left, our neighbours, flooded first..' but all the time my eyes are focussed on the wooden seat on which they are perched: it is beginning to sag alarmingly and to pull away from the side of the hull, not because its passengers are heavy but because this boat is very elderly and much weakened by years of neglect. I can see the headlines, *'Bishop overboard with archdeacon'*. The situation is saved by early arrival at the house where we disembark in the conservatory.

As we splash through the flooded rooms, they are aghast. They can't believe we're still living here. They can't believe that the community seems to have been totally forgotten. We feel grateful for their sympathy and for their having made the effort to come and see for themselves. And Bishop Peter is not just here to goggle, he's here to gather information which he will pass on in a report to his fellow bishop, the Bishop of Wakefield, episcopal Parliamentary spokesman in the House of Lords – where there are some eighteen bishops – who in turn will lobby ministers. Things should start to happen.

Bishop Peter's visit highlights the absence of the EA. This is what their head-honchos should be doing: we know they're flat out dealing with the crisis but a visit from a senior manager to see the extent of the damage to our homes, to commiserate, be brave enough to say, 'Look we're sorry, we've cocked up but this is what we're going to try and do now', all this would have demonstrated real leadership and would have been so much appreciated. Instead I sense the EA are afraid. They've miscalculated. They were complacent and hopelessly unprepared. In response they hunker down safe in their offices. To compensate they spew out online weather information and flood alerts but there are never any boots on the ground. No troops, certainly no generals at the front. We feel like the soldiers in the First World War deeply resenting the top brass who never visited the trenches, had no idea of the living conditions of the men they sent over the top. It brings to mind Siegfried Sassoon's poem, *The General*:

> '*Good morning, good morning!*' *the general said*
> *When we met him last week on our way to the line.*
> *Now the soldiers he smiled at are most of 'em dead,*
> *And we're cursing his staff for incompetent swine.*
> '*He's a cheery old card*', *grunted Harry to Jack*
> *As they slogged up to Arras with rifle and pack.*
>
> *But he did for them both by his plan of attack.*

Chapter 6

SOLO

*Away for the night, staying with great friends on the edge
of the Quantocks. I met Sam years ago when we were both
at I.C.I. While I went off to do the elvers he went on to
become very senior in the company, one of their top fliers. In
their lovely house we are warm, spoiled, wonderfully looked
after and fed delicious meals. Their kindness and generosity
boundless. Like being in a five star hotel. Lucy does all our
washing and stocks me up on food to take back, small portions
read-cooked for when Utta's away. Wild night of weather.
Go for a good run in the lanes, lots of uphill, rain clearing
away after nearly an inch or more. I sleep like a log, the best
in weeks. Head back home for Utta to start packing and get
ready. She leaves on Tuesday.*

For several months now Utta has been planning a trip back
to Australia to see family and friends. It's something she tries
to do every three or four years. She has lived in England now
for nearly forty years, longer than she's lived in Australia; she's
been very happy here, feels a sense of belonging to this part of
the world. And yet every now and then like a migratory bird
she feels compelled to go back to reconnect with what is for

her the essence of Australia: the light, the smells, warmth, bird sounds. That sense of well-being. And when she says 'I feel I've got to go', I know this is something very personal and she must go alone.

Utta's father was from the German-speaking part of Czechoslovakia known as Sudetenland, her mother from Neumunster, a town north of Hamburg. After the war they wanted to make a fresh start in life with their two small daughters. Utta's father, Arno, had been taken prisoner by the Americans in Normandy in 1944 and spent two years as a POW in the southern states of Louisiana and Alabama, some of the best years of his life, he'd say, where he was well treated. 'The food they threw away,' he used to say, 'would have fed us for weeks back home.' During this time he also received full medical and dental care. It was a glimpse of the New World and he wanted some of it. They applied for emigration to several countries and were just about to set sail for Canada when the children went down with chicken pox, so missed their slot. Much of life is about chance: very soon after they heard that their Australian application had been accepted. So in 1954 they boarded an Italian ship, the *Fair Sky*, for their life down under. Something I've always noticed is that Utta's memories from this point on in her life – she was seven years old when they left – are much more vivid than of her life up to then in Germany. In the Mediterranean they took on Maltese emigrants, she was dazzled by the brightness and colour of their clothing, intrigued too by the delousing sessions which she witnessed, peeping through the inner port holes of the sick bay where lice were being removed individually, picked off by hand.

On arrival they were placed in a reception camp for immigrants on the outskirts of Sydney. Life was not easy. Three years after they'd arrived Utta's mother who was pregnant with her third child was obliged to spend six months in hospital – she'd lost her first child – and as her father, Arno, was now long distance lorry driving, Utta and her sister were taken in by friendly neighbours in the street, Uncle Vick and Auntie Evelyn. Vick was half Chinese and had been educated in mainland China. Utta and her sister, Barbara, remember 'he was tall, high cheek-boned with fine eyes, very handsome and smelled of sandalwood.' He was married to Evelyn, very English, small and petite, often in bed propped up on hydrangea blue pillows. She made their breakfast, always soft boiled eggs and 'soldiers', with toast and home-made blackcurrant jam. He did the evening meals, cooking Chinese, wonderful food. They were in their fifties, their children grown up and gone; they heaped love and kindness on these two small girls, Utta a leggy ten year old, Barabara just five with wonderful auburn hair. Vick was retired by then but would help the Chinese community, often market gardeners, with their accounts. Shadowy figures would turn up at the back of the house, their hair in a pigtail, dressed in faded blue dungarees, their sing song language carrying through the rooms along with the click of the abacus.

Shortly after Utta's brother Michael was born, her parents rented a small holding nearby on which they kept chickens, a Jersey cow, a pig. And a goat that ate their socks on the line. Utta would help with milking Goldie and remembers the special warm smell of the animal, the softness of the udder and the ping of the milk in the pail. Her mother made butter and cream from the rich milk. Each winter they butchered the pig with the help of neighbours, keeping the blood in order to make sausages. Utta loved all this, even thought she might be a butcher. In the holidays in her teens she found work on a neighbouring flower farm. Her best memories were the sweet peas; there was a certain way of handling them, bunching them as you picked. At tea break they'd be given black tea, cheese and fresh white bread in the packing shed full of the flowers. A fragrant heaven.

Of such memories we are made.

TUESDAY JANUARY 21ST

There have often been times in our married life when we've been apart for a few weeks for trips like these or for business reasons and always found this kind of separation positive, refreshing. We both enjoy our own company for short spells. This time it is somehow different. Flood-affected. Utta has almost finished her packing, she's travelling light with just one small suitcase. All goes well till around mid-morning when she discovers she's lost her address book with all her Australian contacts in it – like gold dust to her. Almost as bad as losing tickets or passports. We rummage through rooms, on shelves, but in all the chaos it's like looking for a needle in a haystack. It has really rattled her.

We have lunch in the conservatory. Churned by the flood, emotions that have been submerged well up and this last meal together takes on added poignancy as if we were parting for ever or making our last goodbyes. 'If anything happens to me, you must know that I've been very, very happy with you.' It's all very over-emotional, almost comical, clasping hands across the table, over the soup, legs thrust out on stools above the flood water. And yet it's heartfelt. Then, as we are leaving, loading the boat with luggage and bags, she becomes diverted by trying to right the water butt that has toppled over outside the kitchen window. I am fraught and tense; we are running late. I snap at her and immediately feel awful. I apologise but it rips up the feeling that had been between us. I'm aware how unsettling this all is, not just our parting, but for Utta leaving the house behind in its wounded state.

There is however soon a restorative: a great welcome from our grandchildren in London on our way to Heathrow and Utta's flight. The youngest has just discovered he can emit a piercing scream, copied, his Mummy says, from a three year old in the playground. It sounds like a cockatoo being plucked. Officially it's called exercising his lungs.

Alone now and on my way home next day I drive

by way of Oxford to see Emily in her Oxfam offices. At a complicated roundabout with multiple exits I realise, as I wait for the lights to change, that I'm in the wrong lane. I reckon if I reverse a little I can squiggle into the right one. As I make my surreptitious manoeuvre there's a sharp blast on the horn from the vehicle behind. I freeze. In the rear view mirror is a police car. I sit heart pounding, half expecting the tap on the window and the 'May I see your driving license, please sir...' But the lights change and they obviously have better fish to fry, roaring past me and off in another direction. I can just imagine them as they whizz past,

'Another old bugger who's forgotten how to drive, gord 'elp us!'

I feel greatly relieved, also incredibly old and stupid. Also very glad Utta wasn't in the car with me – this would have merited a severe ticking off. Emily restores my nerves with cake and coffee in the Oxfam coffee shop. It is a wonderful tonic to see her and to chat. And to feel proud of her. I depart feeling soothed and ready for anything. I note that I've written in my diary that my aims on return are to 're-build, re-establish and re-invigorate.' Can't quite remember what that's all about but we're obviously ready for action.

THURSDAY JANUARY 23RD

V. cold last night as no Ut to share the bed. Woke around 1-ish cold as a morgue. Lay there trying to get warm. Pile on blankets, a hat and thin blanket around shoulders. Much better. Read *Merivel* for half an hour or so. And then to sleep again. Holly pops over this morning to make sure I've not floated away. She says almost fiercely, 'I said to Utta I'd check up on you every day while she was away.' I feel very honoured. A distinctive figure in her waders which are far too big for her. But she has such an eye for colour. Today it's her sweater. Like a bright flower coming down the road.

Next day there is a text message from Utta on my phone.

Incredibly her little Tesco pay-as-you-go mobile seems to work perfectly twelve thousand miles away. The message is in Utta's best example of minimalist crypto-speak: few vowels, no punctuation, no verbs. Just a series of bullet points from which I deduce she has safely arrived and on her way to a friend's farm in northern New South Wales. Even through these few shards of text, I can sense her joy at being there, like a plant warming to the sun.

I have acquired a fridge. Both of ours have flooded and drowned. It's on loan from Roddy and Holly. Positioning such an item in a normal world might have been a matter of some debate, whether to have it there by the sink or over there by the door and it might have taken days to decide. Here in the flood, it's dead simple: it has to be off the floor and out of the water, so it has to go right there on the kitchen table and it can't be too far away from the one plug in the house above the cooker because there's only a limited length of cable. I take great delight in gaffer taping a pole to the side of the fridge which holds the cable up out of the way of normal traffic, i.e. my head. With a fridge I now have somewhere to store food. I feel this is a major breakthrough.

★★★★★

As the days on my own tick by a kind of routine begins to emerge. Breakfast early on the bathroom floor listening to the *Today* programme, calls from members of the family to see how I'm doing. Time spent in the make-shift office next door doing admin or writing letters to people in the council or the government to highlight our situation here – all of us who've flooded are doing the same. Often a call from outside, a figure standing at the door to the conservatory, someone popping in for a chat and a coffee, news of the flood and of the world beyond. Then it's back upstairs to carry on with the tidying, creating some sort of order in the bedrooms where everything has been piled. Now that I'm on my own, I am aware that I've begun to talk to myself – more than I do normally. It's partly for company, to infuse some human sound into this silent sea-cave of a house. It's also to motivate myself to create some sort of order in the perpetual muddle, 'First we've got to … and then there's the …' Curiously I find myself using 'we', as if the Voice is in charge driving the bloke inside. After lunch I read – again on the bathroom floor where it's warm. I've finished Rose Tremain's *Merivel*, a wonderful book, such humanity in its characters. I record it in my reading log and give it three ticks – my highest award. Now I'm on Artemis Cooper's biography of Patrick Leigh Fermor. Another spell of tidying, or making small improvements about the place. Before too late, as it's getting dark, I run down-river for exercise and to see if there is any change in the flooded moor. Despite all the damage it's done to us, I love it, forgive it for its wild beauty. It's a timeless landscape.

In the evenings I am asked out for supper. People have been very kind and it's got to the point where I have to ring-fence the odd night to be able to have an evening in on my own. When this happens, I still cook in the kitchen on the tilting gas stove and carry it upstairs. At this hour there'll be drifts of phone calls, family, friends calling from all over the country, people I've perhaps not spoken to in ages.

Strange though it might seem, this is not a bad existence. I am cocooned by the flood, almost institutionalised by it like a prisoner in jail. There are times when I almost feel guilty that I am retired, that I don't have to worry about work, about orders that I can't fulfil because of the flood, customers who can't get to my door to buy my goods. This is the case for so many small businesses round here. For them these last few weeks have been ruinous.

However there is a piece of voluntary work which, because of the flood, I've fallen way behind with. This is the Kingfisher Award Scheme, a small charity, originally conceived by poet laureate Ted Hughes, to help primary school children learn about wildlife and its links to farming. The key part of it are the Field Days when the children study a particular habitat in small groups – it might be an orchard, a meadow, an area of wetland. As they explore and learn about different parts of the habitat, they do so guided by specialists who also have to be good communicators. It's outdoor learning, learning by the discoveries they make themselves. They love it. Underlying it all, the aim is to open their eyes to the natural world around them: fewer and fewer children seem now to play outside in fields and woods. It's often regarded as dangerous or the spaces have gone. Increasingly they are closeted inside with the TV and computer games; recent research found some 10% of under fours were put to bed with a tablet computer to play with as they fell asleep. Not surprising there is a growing disconnect between children and the natural world around them.

The scheme is more than just a farm visit for following the Field Day, when they go back to the classroom, the children work together over several weeks, building a display based on their Field experience, drawing on all they've learned. These displays are exhibited and judged at a special Prize Day held in a barn on a farm in the summer term. One great attraction to the schools is that the whole thing is free. This year I'm hoping to use an ancient flower meadow which holds a whole new set of possible topics: barn owl, pond dipping, pollination.

For Utta and myself, it's been a voyage of discovery, one of the main themes of our retirement. It's also taken us to Rome and Paris where I've run marathons to raise funds for the scheme. Above all we've gained so much from it, learned about the wildlife of the Levels from the many gifted naturalists here in Somerset and made many new friends. But it's the children themselves that make it. They come in all shapes and sizes of primary school age, mostly between seven and eleven. In many ways, especially on Field Days, it's been like watching our own grandchildren: their absorption when dissecting a barn owl pellet, wonder when seeing a dragonfly close up; or lifting a net full of creepy crawlies from a pond with a 'Wow'.

Over the years some forty schools around Somerset have taken part. This year I'm way behind with the organisation.

I've managed to book my schools but that's about it. With internet connection still down and the landline not working, progress is even slower. It's time for action, I tell myself. Even though it takes up most of the morning I make an expedition to the nearest hardware store and buy 50 metres of phone extension cable. Plugging one end into the only phone jack above the water line, I carry the landline phone upstairs to my makeshift office in Emily's room and connect the other end. I am just about to try it out when it rings. Bizarrely it's someone wanting to know the price of elvers. Now I gave up my involvement in elvering sixteen years ago; it's almost as if the call has been lodged in the ether all that time and now suddenly, uncorked by the flood, flushed through. Like a message in a bottle cast up on a beach.

And anyway I have no idea of the price of elvers.

★★★★★

With so many wires from phone and electrical cable now running up the stairs I happily hammer nails into the woodwork and walls with impunity, looping the wires over doors and pictures in an effort to support their growing weight, lashing them together like training some rampant vine or wisteria. Normally one would never dream of abusing the walls and woodwork in this way, but the flood has changed the mind-set: the house is wrecked anyway, it's expediency that counts, if it improves our living conditions, then it's fine.

The other discovery is that as one move things, especially smaller objects, putting them into boxes to take upstairs, one suddenly sees them afresh. We have lived with them, amongst them and over time we almost cease to see them; they've become part of the landscape of home. Handling them anew brings them into back into focus, releasing a flood of memories.

It happens today as I'm removing all but the most essential items from the shelf above the cooker in the kitchen. I pick up a kitchen string dispenser, made from a coffee drum, the string fed out through a hole in the lid. When you come to the end of your string, you are greeted by a little note glued to the bottom of the drum which reads, 'Sorry, out of stock'. We've had it and used it for over thirty years. A Christmas present to us from my niece, Henrietta, when she was about twelve. It captures all her quirky individuality, her humour which we loved in her. As I hold it, I am suddenly overcome with emotion.

At the end of the 1990s, by then just thirty something, she was diagnosed with cancer. She lived with it, fought it for six whole years. Although there were long periods of well times, it was always there, shadowing her. In her battle she seemed to find herself, find a courage and strength she perhaps never knew she'd had. She showed such bravery, never moaned or complained or self-pitied. She was always so loving and so giving. An inspiration – a heroine to all of us.

She was also one of the funniest people I've ever known. A wonderful sense of humour, spontaneous, irreverent, quick as a flash and with the most infectious laugh, it could lead off into fits of giggles and render her and all those about her utterly helpless. I remember once when she and her brother, Alexander, were staying with us in the holidays, taking them elver fishing on the river bank. She got stuck in the mud so I, the irritable uncle, went in to get her and I got stuck too – then Alexander got stuck; in the end we just lay in the mud and cried with laughter. I think her wellies are still there.

She had a great talent for caricature, for capturing the essence, which spilled over into the sketches and drawings she made – I've just put one in the box to take upstairs – usually of thin, smiley people, very perky, with a vibrant energy to them. People would ask her to do place names for weddings. We treasure them because they were so essentially her. And these drawings would be sprinkled through her letters and cards. She wrote lots, a great communicator; connecting with people was a theme through her life: notes, messages, thank yous, welcome backs. She wrote as she spoke, hot off the press, the page scattered with asterisks, exclamation marks, dashes. Or perhaps in the corner a little watercolour of a flower or a plant. When you hold one of these letters, draw it from the file, you can still feel its latent energy, the life in it – like holding a bumble bee.

Undoubtedly the best thing that happened in her life was marrying a really good man. In him she found a friend, a soul mate and an anchor. And she found real love and happiness to the end of her brief life.

★★★★★

Wade up to Roddy and Holly for lunch of rabbit pie. Sense how stressed Holly is. Much talk of how they will handle next step, whether to leave or not. The other subject of conversation topic is appearance of rats; they've begun to see them outside near the woodshed. Tell them about my attempts to organise the rubble upstairs, how I feel the need to create some order in all this chaos. Then (after a glass of wine) and further pontificating I wade home to discover that I've left one slipper and my coat behind which Holly has to bring over!

Read after lunch then spend an hour or two starting to sort the chaos in the bedrooms, restacking, packing tight against the walls. My aim is to have them habitable in case the family want to come and stay. It's like a huge jigsaw puzzle and totally absorbing but like any puzzle it needs to be left for a while and approached again fresh.

As it's getting dark I change to go for a run. I need waders to cross the road and reach the river bank where I then change into running shoes and set off down river. I have my head torch if I need it but the eyes quickly accustom to the dark. In normal times Poppy is my running companion, we must have run thousands of miles criss-crossing this moor and beyond. I hardly ever have to call her as she uses me as a moving centre point around which to explore. Tonight, on my own, the dark is soft and private. The wind has dropped but a breeze drives small waves against the bank on my left piling up more sticks, fence posts and flotsam onto the shore line. It has the feel and smell of running by the sea. On the right the river coils by, squeezed by eddies and boiling with currents. After the weekend rain I can still see where it has spilled over into the moor. Great stretches, some fifty metres long where the river bank has subsided over the years, the grass flattened by the waterfall. Put together, these over-spills would make up a sizable river. In places, in the gateways, it's subsided by half a metre. It gets worse every time there's flooding but nothing is ever done to repair the bank. Mainly because no one ever comes to look; no boots on the ground. It's all done by remote.

When I reach the pumping station I'm on surer footing and can settle into a steady pace along the track to Midelney and up to Drayton. All my life I've loved running, the rhythm and feeling of freedom, the wellbeing it gives. My childhood heroes were Roger Bannister and the great Australian middle distance runner, Herb Elliott. I love the simplicity of running, all you need is a pair of shoes and not even that if you're running on a beach. When you are fit and running well, it's like flying. It's my yoga. I feel soothed and de-stressed after a good run. But it's also a wonderful way to explore a new area, a new country. Wherever we travel I take my runners. Just occasionally I have got into trouble. Like the time Utta and I were following in the footsteps of my parents in southern India, visiting Ootacamund or 'Ootie', a popular hill station in the time of the Raj, seven thousand feet up in the Nilgiri hills. It was where my mother had ended up after her trek out of Burma in '42 and where my brother was born. On this occasion I was intending to do some early morning training for a forthcoming marathon, with some speed work around the edge of the old race course which still lay deep in shadow. Suddenly like a rough blanket a large pack of wild dogs I hadn't seen rose up as one from where they'd been sleeping and came straight for me, led by a big brute of a beast. I turned and fled for the exit gate, breaking several speed records in the process. To anyone watching it must have looked hilarious but for me it was utterly terrifying.

I first began running properly, 'cross country' we called it, at prep school in the 1950s. We used to run in a group following the master in charge, down narrow lanes through dense woodland often to a river which we forded by forming a human chain, arms outstretched, water sometimes up to our waists, a great excitement. The custom was that after running for a while we'd stop and wait for the runners at the back to catch up. There was a boy called Mills, short, round and overweight. Mills was always last. A farmer's son. Mills was not to be hurried. He was his own man. He had obviously worked out that if he had to run, then he'd do it on his own terms. So he plodded gently along at the back. His pace never changed, it was Slow unless, urged on by an increasingly apoplectic master, he'd deliberately change gear down into Dead Slow. On finally catching up, as abuse and exhortation rained down upon him, he never said a thing in defence, never complained nor gasped for breath. Only a little smile now and then showed that he was in control of the situation, perhaps the first of us all to discover Passive Resistance. And Mills had a secret weapon. After games, at tea each day we were allowed to supplement the basic fare of bread, butter and jam provided – rationing had not long ended – by drawing 'tuck', stores from home, kept in large tins in a heavily padlocked cupboard and which we were encouraged to share with those on our table. My mother's fruit cakes, raw in the middle, were hugely popular but when Mills went to draw his tuck, it was the Star Event: we waited with baited breath for he'd produce cans of clotted cream from the family farm, the best rich thick clotted cream that I've ever tasted or ever will. And as we waited breathless to be offered some, Mills would look quietly up and down the table with his little smile, a king, savouring his power over us all. However fast we might be able to run, we fawned and toadied before him, like obsequious courtiers desperate for favours. For our share of cream.

★★★★★

Back to hot bath after the run then wade down to supper with Chris and Rita at the Anchorage. They've been very kind, this is the third time I've been there for a meal. Good natters and laughs, much red wine and a delicious mushroom risotto. Rita is such a good cook. Suggest she could serve takeaways through her kitchen window which is right by where the tractor waits to pick up passengers returning home in the evening.

Just figured out the text from Utta which came this morning. It ended with TC. What the hell is TC, I've been wondering. It couldn't have anything to do with Travellers Cheques, she didn't take any; I've been chewing at it all day, like a clue in the crossword. Then it suddenly came to me: TC equals Take Care. So now I know. And so to bed.

This morning, the old moon, a curl of silver reflected on the lake outside that was the lawn. Send a text to Utta, describing it, and sign off, Robinson Crusoe. Another man by the water.

People have been very kind with so many invitations to meals that I have to use my calendar so as not to double book; I catch myself sounding like some practised socialite, 'No, I'm sorry I'm out then, what about Thursday evening?' When you are on your own, it is so good to have something to look forward to, quite apart from good company and food. It also makes me set targets to get things done each day, lends structure to the chaos. This leads to more muttering and self-admonishment, 'Right, so we're out tonight, let's try and get that corner sorted before we go.' I keep wondering who this 'we' is I keep referring to.

SATURDAY JANUARY 25TH

Lunch in Muchelney with Biddy and Paul whom haven't seen since the fateful afternoon over three weeks ago when it all started. Allow plenty of time as it's nearly a mile to wade and haven't done this before. Take a backpack with extra warm kit. The deepest stretch is at the far end near Graham and Helen's

School Farm, well up to the waist. This is where, years ago in the 1920s in a similar big flood, Graham's grandfather was on his way back from delivering the milk churns by horse and cart when the cart, much lighter without its load, suddenly started to float and swing in the shafts causing near panic to the poor creature.

With deep ditches either side, I have to stay in the centre of the road which I can't see so have to judge the middle. Find it helps to keep an easy pace and the legs spaced wide to maintain a good solid base. Enjoyable lunch with Biddy and Paul, their neighbour, Sally, and the Nightingales. Talk dominated by flood matters, exchange of news, grumbling about the E.A. but great fun. Like a gathering of habitants from scattered islands, the contrast in our situation is again underlined: my preoccupation is with a flooded house, while for them it's the daily struggle getting off the island. Leave to wade back before it gets dark. Wind has got up, blowing waves across the road. Go very carefully through the deepest part. Grey light, billowing clouds; tall rushes line the hedge, their tips silver grey streaming like pennants in the wind. Wild but stunning scene. Enjoy the adventure.

From the visit I learn that Muchelney church has become a focal point, a depot for food and parcels, a shelter for the Fire Crews operating the boat service into Langport. Perhaps most important a meeting place for the community with a meal provided after the Sunday service. It's fitting that the church and others like it standing with their strong towers like beacons around the moors are being used in such a way. The flood has given them new life and meaning.

Inside Muchelney church the panels of the ceiling are painted the entire length of the nave with a unique series of bosomy angels. Many are bare breasted as they look down through clouds and stars, long captions trailing from their mouths like flags, 'Good will towards men' and 'Praise the Lord'. They radiate a happy innocence and joy like some early religious cartoon. Dating from the early 1600s what is a mystery however is how they survived the forbidding eye of the protestant church and the iconoclastic years of Cromwell's Puritans. Possibly they were hidden, covered or painted over. But there is another theory suggested by Catherine Denny, the church caretaker: it was the flood that saved them. And it is very plausible. One can imagine Cromwell's men on their way 'to sort those paintings,' but the approaching party of horsemen forced to turn back, the road impassable in the flood; Muchelney island defending itself from outsiders. And by the time the waters receded, things had moved on.

★★★★★

To supper with Susan and Tony Ogilvy in East Lambrook, a mile or so beyond Kingsbury. We sit on low chairs in front of a large wood burner with a glass of wine. All the world seems well. Tony tells me that for several years the stream that runs past the bottom of the garden used to flood, one year so badly that it ripped through the house and all their neighbours' properties. It was evident that increased run-off from the new dual carriageway on the A303 nearby was backing up when it encountered the narrow archway beneath the old bridge. The aperture in the area of the bridge needed to be enlarged to prevent this happening. The locals could see exactly what was happening each time a flood occurred. As the council refused to take responsibility, the local community decided that the only way to get something done was to form a committee of their own to put pressure on the authorities, which they did and won. 'That's the only way to do it', Tony says. 'The combined effort, and using all the different skills that you find people have in a community.' I make a mental note of it; perhaps we can do the same in Thorney.

Tony tells me about his own family. His father was Polish, they were big landowners before the war in eastern Poland. It took four days to ride round their estate. At the outbreak of war his father fought with the Polish Cavalry on one of his own horses. Later he joined the resistance, the underground fighting forces but was captured by the Russians. He spend forty days packed into a cattle truck designed to take a dozen cattle now carrying sixty prisoners to the Gulag in Siberia where he worked down a platinum mine; so cold in winter in the back of the open lorry taking them to work that they froze together and had to be chipped apart. For recreation they made chess men out of stale bread. After two and a half years, when Russia became our ally, he was released and somehow managing to get to England where he joined the RAF (his brother was flying Mosquitos) and survived the war as a Coastal Command pilot. And met Tony's mother.

I listen enthralled. You couldn't invent a more extraordinary story of how men could survive such conditions, nor the ruthlessness of Stalin's Russia. And yet, as Susan adds, he was an example of the strength of the human spirit: one of the kindest, warmest, most loving of men, a wonderful father, never embittered by what he'd been through.

In fact both Tony and Susan both have remarkable parents.

Over supper conversation turns to Susan's childhood and upbringing in a close and happy family. Her father is Donald Easten, now in his mid-nineties, the last surviving officer of the battle of Kohima in April 1944, one of the most fiercely-fought battles and a turning point in the fight against the Japanese. Kohima was a sleepy hill station in north east Nagaland on the Indian-Burmese border. It was where my father crossed into India two years earlier in '42, he'd even stayed with the District Commissioner Charles Pawsey and played tennis on the court that was to become the focus of the battle. In '44, a Japanese division, some 15,000 strong, had advanced by stealth through the jungle with the aim of cutting the main Allied supply line and taking Kohima as a high base from which to forge into India. They were prevented from doing so by a tiny, motley garrison force consisting of only 1,500 men including cooks and medical orderlies; amongst them Donald Easten's D Company of the 4th Battalion of the Royal West Kents.

Kohima was to become something of a Stalingrad, 61 days of the most intense, savage fighting, often at close quarters, hand-to-hand for weeks until final relief in June. For his bravery in action Donald Easten received the MC.

Some months earlier Susan had invited me over to meet her father, a delightful man, still in remarkable shape mentally and physically. He talked about the battle, its savagery, the desperate shortages of ammunition, food and water. He described how they were provisioned by air and how the water containers would burst on impact. He described too the extraordinary bravery of one of his men, Corporal John Harman, in his D Company who charged an enemy machine gun position on his own, knocking it out with a grenade. The next morning, again alone, armed only with rifle and fixed bayonet, Harman attacked and wiped out another Japanese position that was digging in. This time he was severely wounded on his way back and died in Donald's arms. For his gallantry he was awarded the V.C.

Donald told me that Harman was from Lundy Island and had fought in the Spanish Civil War where he'd been told by a fortune teller that he'd live well into his old age. This had deeply impressed him and he really believed in his own sense of immortality. He'd say to Donald as they were being shelled by the Japs, 'Don't worry, you'll be safe with me'. Donald would point out as they crouched for cover that this was 'complete poppycock' as a shell might just as easily land on him and spare Harman. When word got back to Lundy of Harman's death, it was traditional in those days amongst country people to tell the bees of important events, births, marriages, deaths. As Harman was a keen beekeeper, they went to tell his bees. But the hives were empty. As if they knew already.

On his 90th birthday Susan and Tony took Donald back to Kohima to revisit the battlefield and old memories, a poignant experience that meant a huge amount to him. At the site of the battle now stands an epitaph, one of the most moving, carved in stone:

When you go home,
Tell them of us and say,
For your tomorrow,
We gave our today.

SUNDAY JANUARY 26TH

The water's going down. Could this be the end of it? Soon I can start to pump out the garden. Busy morning with lots of phone calls in and out. More improvements upstairs, rearranged the new office and another good session tidying Ol's room. Invited to very good Sunday lunch with John and Becky Couts by the mill, joined by Holly and Roddy and Rita and Chris. Usual flood talk, comparing water levels, the damage, insurance companies and generally how we're handling the chaos of life, all seasoned with a degree of black humour. But today the mood is noticeably low, depressed by the never-ending drudgery, trying to fit work and domestic life round this endless muddle; there is talk of moving out, finding rooms to rent for a while.

'And how are you doing on your own, Michael; are you thinking of leaving?' someone asks.

'Well, I feel a bit of a fraud in all this. I'm retired so I haven't got work to worry about. I've got space upstairs, I've got hot water. It sounds terrible but I'm actually very happy.'

At this point, were this a film or a play, there might be a sound off stage, the deep tolling of a bell or dark strains of music – as in Jaws – to presage something ominous about to happen. When pride or self-confidence, man's hubris, offended the gods of ancient Greece it was usually punished.

That evening I am in the kitchen getting supper. The depth of water is still about seven inches next door in the old part of the house but here in the kitchen there's barely an inch on the floor so it's a pleasure to be in wellies and not to have to struggle into waders. I'm sipping a glass of red wine. I have music on the radio. I'm feeling happy, looking forward to a good read with my meal. Despite the flood, life is not all bad. Suddenly there's a slight noise from the door through to the old part. As I glance in the direction of the sound, an enormous rat, the largest I've ever seen, slithers round the door. His fur is wet, he must have swum in from outside, his tail as thick as a cord. Nose to tail he must be at least a foot and half long. We do not stop to talk. He's on a mission. He wants warm and dry, possibly even a hot bath. I hear myself, a great gasp of horror from deep, deep down inside me, expressed in a shuddering intake of shock, 'Oh my God'. He slithers across the kitchen and through the door into the corridor – and this is what's so terrifying – heads for upstairs. Rats outside, that I can bear. But the thought of sharing my living space with a creature that size is unimaginable. It's all over in seconds but it leaves me severely shaken. What was all that about not wanting to leave! It suddenly sounds like a bloody good idea.

Forgetting supper, I follow his trail. Once through the hallway he'd have had two choices: he could have gone left upstairs, or turned right into my old office where the window is open. It's just possible he went back out that way. Armed with a stick I scour the rooms upstairs, banging on doors and walls to flush him out. But nothing. Wherever possible I close doors, forming bulkheads, then pack all the food on the breakfast shelf outside our bedroom into plastic boxes. Certainly not going to have him sharing my muesli. While I'm doing all this, I resolve to ask Glen in the morning if he can move the door from the old office up to the half landing on the stairs to form a permanent barrier – and it'll help retain any warmth upstairs.

After much whacking of the bedclothes to make sure he's not taken refuge in them, it's cautiously to bed and a fitful sleep. Much chastened.

Retribution of the gods. By rat.

Chapter Seven

INTERLUDE

*Another cryptic text message from Utta in Australia. I gather
that she's now in Sydney, seeing friends, exploring old
haunts. And blissfully happy. Space for herself. Meanwhile
an anonymous text from an unknown person demands,*

*'When she coming? Please give flight details.' I have no
idea who it's from, nor if the 'she' even refers to Utta. Roused
to protective status like the castle gatekeeper calling 'Who goes
there', I text back guardedly,*

'Please identify yourself.'

*It turns out to be Mike, her brother, wanting to know
when she's arriving in Tasmania.*

MONDAY JANUARY 27TH

No serious rain now for a few days. Water level definitely
dropping. It is out of the main house, about four inches in
the old part. Get in touch with insurance company and it
is arranged that they'll come down on Thursday. Good,
productive morning. No sign of the rat. Though expect to see

it at every turn. Glen will come over when he can and fit the door on the stair landing. Started to pump out the garden, and the clean up outside. Rake up barrow loads of foul smelling weed and decaying vegetation floated in from the moor mixed through with rotting apples and tip it into the river, from whence it came. Particularly thick where it's been trapped round the back. Perfect habitat for the rodent population, though judging by the holes in the side of the garden shed they've already made headquarters in there, beside the little freezer. Start to pull up the kitchen floor and the carpet in the sitting room. In its waterlogged state it is incredibly heavy and I'm going to need help. Harry Osmond who lives up the road towards Kingsbury and where we've parked our van very kindly offers to come on Wednesday and give me a hand. He's going to bring his car jack too so that we can raise the heaviest furniture to get the carpet out from underneath.

Simon Taylor phones to say that John Osman, leader of Somerset County Council and his deputy, David Hale, are waiting to be collected at the end of the road. This was arranged shortly after the bishop's visit in response to a salty letter Simon wrote to Osman in which he pulled no punches:

'…Muchelney has received some help. Thorney has not. Friends are crapping into plastic bags because septic tanks are swamped. Phone calls to the local councillor have reportedly been met with comments like, 'What do you expect me to do about it?' Well even the bishop couldn't do a lot but he took the time to come with the archdeacon and listen and see people's pain – it all helps. But you can help if you'd come and listen....'

And signed, 'From the land that local government forgot.'

So here they are. John and David. Two polite, pleasant gentlemen in shiny wellies slightly nervous about the possibility of being harangued and equally nervous about being loaded into my eel boat. Seeing people close up from behind – an angle they're not usually viewed from, reminds one that, whatever their status, we are all simple human beings: glimpses of hasty

dressing, a coat hitched up on a belt. Like viewing the reverse
side of a picture or a tapestry, all the untidy, hidden bits visible.
But more especially my eyes are once again glued to the thwart
seat on which they are both sitting, watching it pull away from
the hull, praying that it's going to hold. It does and we are able
to disembark at the gate as the level has dropped that much. I
show them round inside the house. We slosh through the lower
part, still some four inches deep, but in a way it's a shame that
the main house is now almost clear as it's much less dramatic.
I feel a bit like the safari guide when all the game is asleep
or gone to bed. However when we come to the kitchen I'm
able to give them a graphic account of the visit from the Rat
last night, still very fresh in the memory, which helps enliven
their tour. Detect the odd nervous glance at the door from
whence he came. But they listen closely and sympathetically
and it is good to put names to faces. Returning them to dry
land, Simon, whisks them away for another visit.

To supper with Simon and Jayne. Take running kit and
run from their house through the lanes and orchards behind
Kingsbury, good to run on terra firma, starry night, windless
for once. Back to shower in their house and supper. Lovely
evening with good chats. Talk to them both about forming
a Thorney action group to prevent future flooding along the
lines of the one Tony Ogilvy described on Saturday. Simon
agrees to be the chairman. He will be a great asset as he has the
experience and confidence of working with people in positions
of power and authority. Knows which buttons to press. On
a practical level they very kindly offer to hold any meetings
we have around their kitchen table. Saves us all sitting in our
conservatory having to hold our legs up out of the water.

★★★★★

I am aware that my intake of news, local and national, is as
erratic as the weather. In the morning I listen to the *Today*
programme as I am getting up. Much of it at the moment
devoted to the flooding and to interviews with local MP's. But

our daily delivery of a newspaper has ceased, so I only read a paper when I buy one out shopping. The internet and email are still down despite Roddy's help in trying to reconnect. And whenever I sit upstairs in our bedroom in the evening, wrapped in a rug to catch the news on our ancient telly, it's an instant invitation to fall asleep. I don't think I've seen a single TV news right through. So, apart from the radio, I rely heavily on word of mouth, often from Rod and Hol and phone calls. Even if I was up-to-date on all the news I have a feeling that the flood has made us all more parochial, focussed more than ever on the immediate difficulties of our lives. Too engrossed to think outside of our own predicament. Most of us know that Muchelney has been cut off now for nearly a month, but it's often days later that I hear that other parts of the moor have been flooded. It's almost as if they're foreign countries.

In fact I am only now just beginning to be aware that a major incident has been declared for flood-affected areas of Somerset. I happen to meet Carolyn Roche, our village agent, as she's waiting to board the tractor through the flood. She tells me it's the best thing that could have happened. Apparently it was announced first by Sedgemoor District Council. Somerset County Council then had to follow suit.

'Run by men', she says, 'Always reluctant to shout for help as it looks as if they can't manage.'

Her view is that not declaring an emergency has up to now been a kind of block. The declaration now means that local authorities can organise emergency services to move in, set up evacuation centres and mobilise voluntary agencies. That would explain all those men in yellow jackets I saw when I was in Muchelney for lunch on Saturday. Somewhat uncoordinated, it seemed.

Carolyn's post of village agent is a new one created a few years ago in parts of the West Country. She is looking after some ten parishes, including Muchelney and Thorney, with the aim of helping and giving support to people in rural areas where it's needed, visiting and trying to solve problems and get to people before they need serious help from social service; it's a preventative social brief. It is supposed to be part time but at the moment she is flat out and more than full time. In this flood emergency she has been doing a fantastic job, looking out for us all in this part of the village whilst liaising constantly with Muchelney. She has been our switchboard and communications centre. I can't receive her emails but she calls or pops round to make sure I'm all right and getting information or a share of the tasty ready-meals being left at Muchelney church.

Privately it's been very tough for her too with two small children, getting them back and forth to nursery school. If there's no tractor-ferry, she says she walks up the river bank across from our house, the only way round the flood on foot to get to her car.

Looking back on it, she says, 'At times it was awful, ghastly. On bad days I'd be crying into the wind, making sure the children couldn't see me. All of us slipping over in the mud and wet, the kids crying, wanting to be carried.'

★★★★★

News is also emerging that Owen Paterson, Secretary of State for Energy, Food and Rural Affairs has been in Somerset and visiting the area of Moorland in particular. I know Moorland well from elvering days. A mile or so above Bridgwater, it was a good spot for elvers. I'd park up in a layby by the river and wait for the fishermen to weigh in, several of them came from around there. Many of the houses lie beside or close to the river which bends around the village, surrounded by moors that often flood each year. Though, like us, they have never flooded this badly before. What makes the village particularly vulnerable is that by the time it reaches Moorland the river Parrett, swelled by the rivers Isle, Yeo and Tone is carrying the entire flood water of the surrounding hills. It's a huge volume. And then there is the small matter of the high tide which twice daily reaches this far up-river – blocking the outflow. Nor is it helped by the fact that there is only one very narrow road running through the village from Burrowbridge up-river on the A361 – partially flooded in both directions – down to Bridgwater which is fast becoming the only way out. It must be a nightmare for the residents.

I see them on the evening news. Facing the cameras they are plainly fuming, very angry, watching helpless as their houses fill with water, their livelihoods floating away. Nothing seems to have been done. For far too long they've been left leaderless.

'Why has nothing been done since last year? Why have the pumps just been put in now? We've had no answers. We needed to see this three weeks ago. We did ring them, asked them to bring pumps in, but they didn't listen. Life is stressful, exhausting.'

It's like watching ourselves. Just the sort of things we might have said if anyone had come to speak to us.

Apparently Paterson held a meeting last night with various representative bodies. I heard later from someone who was at the meeting that he was impressive, listened to the evidence, got tough with the E.A, insisting on a plan of action with a deadline. For all that the flood is no respecter of reputations.

Local people interviewed were clearly disappointed; they'd been hoping to speak to Paterson but he wouldn't meet them. Instead, he met with local officials at the Northmoor pumping station near Moorland to announce that he wants to see a 'concrete plan from all interested parties to provide a long-term solution to deal with the flooding and to be submitted within six weeks'. This is good news for us. However, he refused to meet protesters outside and listen to their grievances. Worst of all it was spotted that he was wearing shoes not wellies. The media have seized on this and wellies have instantly become a potent symbol. They were, I learn later, in the boot of his car but as he was given a lift to the meeting by the local MP, Liddel- Granger, he wasn't able

to change into them. That matters not to the public. Wellies
mean 'I'm one of you, I understand you,' they are part of
rural life; shoes belong to the office, the city, to people who
don't understand. It's facile but in this world of visual images
it's vital when emotions are so raw.

Makes one wonder how often people, events through
history have been affected by some similar misconception,
some little detail that became all-important, like the 'donkey
jacket' that Michael Foot wore at the annual wreath laying
ceremony in 1981, seen as highly disrespectful at the time. In
fact it wasn't a donkey jacket, it was a short blue green coat but
the damage to his reputation was irreparable.

Meanwhile, since Martin Hesp's article in the *Western
Morning News* and the bishop's visit, Thorney is now definitely
on the map. We exist. News crews, photographers have found
their way here. They arouse mixed feelings: annoyance on
the one hand, like flies settling on a new carcass and yet also
gratitude for the coverage that brings us to the attention of
politicians and hopefully action. As this house is nearly the
deepest point in the flood and as most don't have waders, I
am happily free from having to give interviews. However
Roddy and Holly, as well as Rita and Chris opposite, are on
the edge of the flood where the parking starts so are frequently
interviewed and photographed.

It is a real eye-opener how quickly material is syndicated
and travels the world. David and Ingrid from Muchelney are
at this time visiting their son in Western Australia. They stop
at a roadside café for a cup of tea in the middle of nowhere
and browsing through the local paper are astonished to see
a picture of Holly wading down the middle of the road in
Thorney, under headline, 'Flooding in Somerset'.

Meanwhile the one photographer who does get to this
house, equipped with waders, is Matilda Temperley whose
grandfather's house is opposite. From a first class science
degree and research into malaria in Africa, she has launched
successfully into a new career in photography. Very photogenic

herself with a radiant smile, she has a good eye and takes striking, atmospheric black and white shots of the flood and its extent. With cameras and lenses draped around her neck at the ready, she pops in for a chat but I sense she's often only half involved in the conversation as she is constantly taking shots as we talk. Some months later, turning the pages of her excellent book of photographs recording the Somerset floods, I came across an image of a stern looking figure in waders standing, his back to the wall, in a flooded room. Poor sod, I think, he looks extremely grumpy, things have obviously got to him.

Then, peering closer, I realise it's me.

★★★★★

As I sip my early morning tea I've started to notice each morning through our bedroom window a conference of jackdaws on the thatched roof of Nick's house, the Old Rising Sun, next door. I think they must be sensing spring and the urge to build nests. Clearing up after the last flood in November 2012 Nick found that each of his chimneys was blocked with nesting material dropped by these birds. He took away eight large bin bags stuffed with knobbly twigs of chestnut, ash and oak, in total probably well over a hundred kilos representing thousands of hours of diligent gathering by the birds over years. Nick gave us four bags of the twigs which have made wonderful kindling. But to prevent it happening all over again wire cones have been placed on all the chimney pots as we have done here.

The jackdaws do not like this, which accounts for the conference. They live in hope. Each morning they visit the chimneypots to see if by chance the wire defences have been removed. At first there's a sort of coffee shop atmosphere, lots of chat, socialising and gossip on the thatched roof as they fly in from neighbouring trees to congregate. Then it's down to business. Working in twos or threes, they hop up onto the chimney stacks, circling round the pots, peering down longingly through the bars of the wire capping as they try to squeeze themselves through. From the general chatter of the earlier gathering there's now a distinctly different sound to their language. Short, sharp calls. Question and answer.

'Any luck?'

'Nope, just the same.'

'How 'bout you?'

'No good, too tight. Sod's blocked them.'

But they don't give up. It's a challenge. Different pairs hop up and try their luck, circle the pots searching for the one weak point that could provide entry and thus a chance to build. Eventually after an hour or so, they fly over to the ash tree opposite and from there depart for the day. There's always tomorrow; they'll be back. I love their perkiness, their busy-ness and in this watery world, suspended above the flood they are a shining example of hopeful determination.

THURSDAY JANUARY 30TH

Good day yesterday. With Harry Osmond's help cleared all the carpets and flooring and piled them on the lawn along with barrow loads of muck, duckweed, apples and flotsam. Feel much happier now, confidant – but not overly so – that it'll be less attractive to the rats. Thought I saw another one a couple of days ago. In the sitting room, much smaller but gave me a nasty fright. But no sign since. Keeping all doors shut between rooms to prevent their encroachment. Where there are cables and wires trailing from kitchen to upstairs, I've cut V-notches in the tops of the doors for the wires to go through so that I can still close the door.

Worked hard all day, a full ten hours. Harry was great. Very kind of him. For supper tinned chicken curry with cabbage on the side. Very tasty. And so to bed! Slept like a log till 2-ish then awake listening to the owls. Rat hunting, I hope. Read Patrick Leigh-Fermor's biography till drop off again.

This morning, Thursday, and the insurance team arrive punctually at 9.30. They are able to wade down the road in their wellies. There are five of them. Show them round first.

They are very professional, they must have seen this sort of thing a hundred times, though it's unusual for them to arrive, through no fault of their own, nearly a month after the event. They make all the right sympathetic noises, lots of clucking and tut-tutting and at the end of the tour the expressions of well-worn phrases almost as if reading from some brochure, 'In this distressing time, you can depend on us to do everything possible...' As Nick, next door, says afterwards, for we share the same insurance company, 'it's a bit like having the undertakers round.' They then hold an impromptu meeting standing in the hallway – there's nowhere to sit, but they must be used to that – working out a plan of action while I give them tea and slices of the very good fruit cake Liz Nightingale brought us. They must have been up very early because most of them have seconds. I'm happy to see there's still some left in the tin.

My job now is to phone the builder, Ed, and have him meet Peter, the company's claims man who suggests he and I can deal direct, no need for a loss adjustor. Nick has to have one of these as his house is listed and the flood has severely damaged the cob walls; they're currently more like porridge than cob. Feel much better about things especially as they made an immediate transfer of funds to our account to keep us going and to allow any necessary purchases.

★★★★★

Tomorrow the cleaning gang will come in to sanitise the flooded area, then install the dryers and humidifiers. I get in touch with Tim, the electrician, with their list of requirements for the three phase supply of electricity and all the related heavy duty cabling which he is happy to install straightaway.

That evening, leaving instructions with the cleaning gang on how to get into the house, I head off to stay the night with Di, my sister, in Wiltshire for we are travelling northward together to a family funeral the next day, picking up Alastair along the way. Over supper at her house we have long natters, reminiscing about Mum and Dad and the cousins. Angela, to whose funeral we are going, was married to our mother's first cousin. There were about eight of them, aunts and uncles and cousins, all roughly of the same generation, all very close and deeply fond of one another. Each year they would visit each other at set times, usually a summer stay followed by a return visit in the autumn. You could have set the seasonal clock by the regularity of these visits. They were meticulously planned, pondered over, preceded by letters and phone calls, with recommendations as to the best route to take, estimated times of arrival. An ascent of Everest could not have been better prepared.

In anticipation of any such visit Mum would write lists of meals and food to serve. She never slept well at the best of times; an impending visit would create nights of insomnia as she worried over menus while Dad snored blissfully beside her.

One after another through the 1990s they have all gone, leaving only Angela, once the youngest, now the last of them all, making her final exit at the great age of 88. A grand innings. It was very good fortune that we had four days in her company when staying with her daughter last September. A forthright but affectionate character, she was in great form and very good company. Very striking, immaculately groomed, wonderful hair, full of spirit, always up for a walk, a visit, a drive. We went mushrooming with her in the fields before breakfast.

As we enter the packed church, one of the cousins whispers loudly to me as I pass their pew,

'We've got something for you' and they indicate a large plastic bag concealing something round and heavy. They know that we've been flooded so without having time to rootle inside, I assume from the look of it that it is probably some kind of camping Portaloo, which could come in very handy. I shall have to wait till the bun fight afterwards to see what's inside. Meanwhile it is, as funerals go, one of the best I've ever been to. A wonderful send-off and celebration of a life with all the family, grandchildren, cousins taking part and performed with great feeling, tenderness and much humour.

Angela would have loved it.

Afterwards, on closer examination the bag contains not a camping loo but a huge cake tin, the size of a kettle drum. And inside an enormous fruit cake which I can tell from a few hastily sampled crumbs is utterly delicious.

On my way back from the funeral there's a phone call from the contractors to report that they're just leaving, everything's been done, they've cleaned the whole of the house downstairs, the dryers and dehumidifiers are on and they'll be back next week to check on progress. It all sounds very efficient. A little too slick. But when I get home I am not prepared for the sheer wall of noise that greets me when I walk inside. It's like being in an aircraft engine testing hangar, or standing in a wind tunnel. Very draughty. Beside each of the blowers is a dehumidifier with an outlet pipe leading into a large container. These need to be emptied like patients' bed pans every few hours. Something else to remember. Each room downstairs has its own set of machines. It's going to be ear plugs in tonight. Definitely. Or switch them off. One advantage is that the noise should deter any inquisitive rat but then I would have thought that about the floodwater. Fortunately Glen is going to fit the door on the half landing very soon which will help against rats and noise. Meanwhile I'm glad the insurance company is paying for the electricity; I've just noticed the digits on the mains board clocking up quicker than a London taxi. What is disappointing is that the 'cleaning' promised by the contractors has little to do with mops and brushes and elbow grease. All they've done is spray a sanitiser like weed killer over the floor which is still covered in duck weed, twigs and silt. Looks rather like a dried-up river bed.

I note that it's the end of January and from the rainfall figures given to me by Sally England, official recorder, at the caravan site down the road in the other half of Thorney, we had over six inches of rain this January. I don't think there's been a wetter one on record. This came on top of twelve in the autumn period October to December. So well over eighteen

inches so far this winter and this doesn't take into account
the rainfall on the hills around – probably twenty four inches
to our eighteen – from which our rivers receive the run-off.
And listening to the weather forecast, there is more to come.
Something to do with the jet-stream which has stuck and
continues to shovel storms and low pressure systems this way
like some unstoppable conveyor belt.

Just heard from Roddy today that someone in Hambridge,
the other side of our West Moor, has been found opening the
sluice gates off the river Isle to save his own property from
flooding. His actions have allowed huge volumes of water
into the moor – the equivalent of a breach in the river bank.
Apparently to open them he had to smash the locks on the
gates first. It wouldn't have caused our flood but it well might
have added to it. Investigations are underway.

MONDAY FEBRUARY 3RD

Oliver down over the weekend to see the house and help me
clear up. A tower of strength. We got a lot done, the drowned
sofas out, skirting boards off, clearing garden and shed. So
precious having him on his own. So proud of him; he's grown
into a good man. And a wonderful Dad. Just loves his little
team. He left about 6-ish last night back to London..

The computer is working but there is still no internet
connection, so no email. In our normal lives we check for
incoming email first thing in the morning, at intervals during
the day and last thing at night. And that's not counting the
time spent sending emails ourselves. I never thought I'd see
ourselves doing this but it has happened very gradually –
probably like the arrival of the motor car, a novelty that became
a necessity. Being without email for over a month would
normally be unthinkable, very frustrating. But when Roddy
asks me incredulously, 'Don't you miss it?' I realise I don't,
not in the slightest. What has really made the difference is the
fact that our lives are already so disconnected, unplugged, by

the flood from the normal daily routines and rhythms. There is no doubt the computer is invaluable in many ways, yet a great deal of what we receive here is unsolicited junk in some form or other with only a sprinkling of proper email letters from friends. Whilst these are wonderful they are never quite the same as receiving a letter in the post, handling the pages, feeling someone's presence through their handwriting, putting them aside to read again and again. Such things have vanished now. We might get one 'old fashioned' letter a year – if we're lucky. Mainly from a friend in Australia who hates computers. Trouble is we can't read her handwriting.

★★★★★

A busy morning of garden clearing, then deskwork, all this mixed in with several callers. In this time of flood it would be quite possible to stand outside in the road in my waders and chat to passers-by all day. Later I return upstairs to try to put some order into the chaos of all those belongings hastily rescued from the flood. For half an hour or so things go well, sorting, making space, consolidating until, as always seems to happen, I get distracted. There's a drawer full of forgotten diaries and notebooks that I'd grabbed from my office desk below. It is years since I looked at them. Picking one of them at random, I open it and kneeling on the landing floor start reading. I find it's the diary I kept in the summer of 1973 as I walked the old pilgrim route to Santiago de Compostela, site of the tomb of the apostle James in north west Spain. The memories flood back.

I was accompanied by an American girl whom I'd met on a kibbutz the year before. She had probably never walked further than to the post office in her life but she was keen to make the journey. She was also tough and uncomplaining, a good companion. And had good legs for walking. While one of the Sunday papers had commissioned a number of pieces for their Travel section, the real motive for both of us was not religious but the sense of adventure, a real journey on foot following an ancient path where thousands had gone before. For me personally there was also the vague notion that walking would help me sort out my life – 'solvitur ambulando, it is solved by walking'– to decide which direction to take next.

We started from Le Puy in the Haute Loire, west of the Rhone valley, one of four gathering points for pilgrims in the old days and set out south west across the rugged hills of the Massif Central. It was toward the end of June and at night we'd expected to sleep out under the stars, 'à la belle etoile'. However there were no stars for it rained incessantly. Instead we sought shelter in barns or ruined buildings. We went to bed soaked and pulled on wet boots in the morning. We might have given up then and there had it not been for the commitment to produce the articles for the paper. There was also another incentive, a deadline: we had to be in Santiago by the beginning of September to allow time to attend a friend's wedding.

Like snails we headed south west through the Cantal and the Monts d'Aubrac, through wild uplands and forest, tiny villages and hamlets half abandoned, the diary full of images and incidents I'd long forgotten: a shepherd in the rain with heavy cagoule, nodding as we passed, 'Vous êtes courageux. Il ne fait pas du beau temps – not nice weather;' fields of wildflowers, sound of water trickling everywhere, the scent of broom; a friendly woman bringing in her cows to the parlour, each one with its own named stall, 'Jacotte, Pivoite, Lilliane.' We crossed into the Lozere, walls of stone, roofs of stone, wet stone tiles shining like coins; sleeping in a grain barn in the wooden grain bin to exclude the howling draught – there were rats there too. And slowly down to Conques, a small village with a magnificent Romanesque church.

Back then in the early 1970s, the pilgrim route wasn't yet signed and waymarked but I'd researched the towns and villages it had passed through so we'd ask or use the large scale French maps to find the 'chemin de St Jacques'. We were helped by the string of tiny chapels, often dedicated to St Roch, one of the pilgrim saints, or decorated with the scallop shell – the symbol of St James that let us know we were on the route. These markers gave us warm reassurance like meeting old friends. Every walking day had its boring bits, its frustrations as we found ourselves heading in the wrong direction or the route overgrown. And yet there were always magic times too, one stretch at least when we'd hit a fine path and get into a good stride, hear the rhythmic thump of boots, the creak of rucksack and feel we were flying.

Nowadays the route to Santiago has become hugely popular again but back then we met only one fellow pilgrim on our entire journey and that was in Conques at the end of that first week. Dennis was French but spoke several languages fluently; he'd been in the diplomatic service but had left to become a priest. On the month break from his theological studies he had decided to walk to Santiago. This was an incredibly tight schedule – far more rigorous than ours – almost requiring him to run all the way. He would have been about thirty, tall, lean, wearing army shorts and beret and carrying an enormous rucksack the size and weight of a small boulder. We got on instantly and agreed to walk together through Figeac and Cahors down to Moissac. He was great company, we laughed and chatted and told stories, shared intimate thoughts and problems as pilgrims have always done down through the ages. He had a deep faith but he never tried to proselytise or preach. Reading the diary I can see that he was the best thing that could have happened to the two of us. Over the week we spent together, by his example we revved up, learned to put in the big miles each day. He was also a fund of knowledge about the churches we saw along the way. Like having our own guide. When we parted in Moissac it was with great sadness, we had shared so much, got to know him so well. As we watched him walk away, we said with feeling, 'There goes the next Pope.' And we meant it.

In Moissac, to restore our fast disappearing funds, we managed to find work on a nearby fruit farm picking peaches for a week. It belonged to two generations of family, the older couple having started the business after the war cultivating a few fields, taking their produce to market by horse and cart. By the time we met them it had grown into a thriving business with many hectares on the banks of the river Tarn.

They were wonderful people, the very salt of the earth: hardworking, thrifty but generous and with huge energy and zest for life. The photos I took of them at that time still hang on the walls here at Willow Cottage and remind me of them every day. Friendships like these were always part of the pilgrimage, especially when pilgrims stopped along the way to work or saw a better way of life and decided to stay. All adding to a great cross-cultural enrichment.

★★★★★

Heading south west towards the Pyrenees, the route took us through the Gers, past Lectoure, Eauze, Aire sur l'Adour. Walking became a way of life, wholly absorbing. Changes in landscape, in crops, stone and architecture, changes in dialect, cheese and bread, gently unfolded beside us. France – and Spain – were then still deeply rural. Shepherds with flocks of sheep filled the paths; horse and carts still gathered hay, rivers powered mill wheels and bakeries produced great round loaves of pain de seigle, rye bread with thick tarry crusts. Each night we cooked on a little camping gaz; we ate well, trying out local specialities, cheeses, bread and vegetables that we bought along the way.

As we passed farms and villages people were always curious and would ask, 'Où est-ce que vous allez comme ça' – where are you heading? When they learned we were pilgrims on our way to Santiago we'd often see in their eyes a wistfulness to drop everything and come too. Down the ages that might well have happened. There's something about the wanderer, the hiker passing with a pack that stirs some ancient, restless longing in us. To be free and out on the open road.

At St. Jean-Pied-de-Port we rested and slept in the lavoir, the wash house, waiting for the weather to clear to cross the Pyrenees. When the mists lifted we followed a path worn into the mountain by the boots of shepherds, smugglers, pilgrims and by Napoleon's troops after the Peninsular Wars. We crossed the frontier without a customs barrier in sight. Dropping through forests of beech to the great abbey of Roncesvalles then onto Pamplona and Estella with its ancient medieval bridge, long as a spine, we headed due west to Santiago, through the Rioja, past Burgos. In Castille we followed the old Roman road, straight as a lance, under a scorching sun through the 'meseta', high uplands of wheat, grassland and shepherds, a wild and empty land. Re-reading the diary I remember that these were some of our best walking days. We were fit and lean and hardened. We were flying along. We'd cook and sleep on the track, waking before dawn to the sound of voices, the squeal of axles and wooden carts as villagers made their way to the fields. We'd walk till midday then eat and conk out fast asleep under poplars that grew in the narrow valleys. When it was cooler, we'd walk again till early evening. By now we were doing twenty to twenty five miles a day. Each night we'd mark our progress on the map and watch the red line inching its way across the north of Spain through Leon, Astorga and Villafranca into Galicia. Dennis would have been proud of us.

As Santiago drew nearer, the camino de Santiago, the pilgrim route, grew stronger, more marked as all the minor routes and tributaries combined to form the one main route. In places broad paths wide enough for an army wound uphill paved with stone slabs worn smooth from the passing traffic of people. In its heyday, in the eleventh and twelfth centuries, Santiago was one of the great pilgrimages of the Christian world, alongside Jerusalem and Rome, attracting more than a quarter of a million pilgrims a year. Yet, the diary reminds me, Galicia was some of the poorest country we'd seen along the way. Tiny hamlets with streets of earth. Carts drawn by oxen. Scenes of threshing in farmyards. Sheepdogs in the hills with chain link collars against attack by wolves. There's a description, one morning sleeping on the track, woken by the men from the village, scythes on their shoulders on their way to mow a field. We watched them working in a row felling the high grass with great rhythmic sweeps. Striking, I remember, were their smiles, happy faces, their sense of camaraderie working together. So different to a bloke on his own, shut in his tractor cab all day.

On the 2nd of September we reached Santiago and its great square, entering the cathedral, a mixture of peace, wondrous carving and religious bling. We climbed to kiss the head of the apostle. The diary notes 'a metallic taste'. It was still the custom then that on completing the journey pilgrims were given three days free meals in the smart hotel on the edge of the great square. We couldn't believe our luck. Rumbling with hunger and armed with our pass from the cardinal's office we approached Reception desk in the hotel, where a polite young lady told us, yes, we were entitled to be fed, but not in the restaurant. No, round the back, up the wooden stairs and in the staff canteen. It was basic fare but still wonderful, especially after juggling two little pots over a single gas flame for forty six walking days over a thousand miles. Later we collected our mail from the Poste Restante and were handed a telegram from our friend. It read cryptically, 'Wedding postponed. Details to follow.' It took just a few seconds to get over the disappointment and realise that the deadline set by the wedding had been the best incentive to have hauled us along the path to the end.

Instead we hitched back to Moissac to pick more fruit with the same family we'd met.

On return home the articles were written and duly published but it is quite clear from the diary that at the end of it all I still hadn't the faintest clue what I was going to do next. But it didn't matter, it had been a memorable walk, unforgettable, a last chance to see an older rural way of life in France and Spain that has largely vanished since.

WEDNESDAY FEBRUARY 5TH

High winds and lashing rain all night. Nearly an inch by morning. On the news, massive storm damage on the coast. Part of the Dawlish line from Exeter to Plymouth that runs along the sea washed away; winds of up to 92mph in the Scillies, and part of Chesil beach in Dorset destroyed. Outside the river running very high again. Pretty sure we're going to see the water back in our houses here in Thorney.

Yesterday afternoon, however, for Prince Charles's visit to Muchelney, it stayed clear. Several of us wandered down to Thorney for a gawp where he was having tea with Mike and Jenny Curtis at Thorney Moor Farm. It's not every day that you catch sight of the future King. Something of an enforced holiday atmosphere especially as so many of the small businesses up and down the road can't operate and so had decided to come along. Met Johnny Leach on the way who said, albeit in remarkable humour, 'not a penny has gone into our till since the beginning of January.' And that's the second year running for him. As the small crowd waited outside the farm for a glimpse of Himself, a helicopter hovered high overhead, no doubt equipped with cameras and image intensifiers so powerful that they could read the label on your shirt, or in my case spot the tomato soup I spilled on my trousers over lunch. When he emerged from the house, HRH was terrific, connected with the crowd, eye contact, looked right at you, right into you, so although there was no time for a chat, you felt as if you'd met him. Politicians would pay good gold for such a gift. When I asked Mike and Jenny Curtis later what it had been like hosting HRH, and if they'd been nervous, they said it had all been so easy, he'd been delightful, interested and interesting, 'It was like talking to your parents' best friend.'

Later I meet Colin and Edwina from the house across the river. They'd been down to see him in Muchelney, getting a lift on the tractor that was being sent to collect him with a large wheel-backed bench on the trailer for him to sit on.

Edwina says, 'On the way down I sat on his throne to keep it warm for him.' I hear later from friends in Muchelney that he'd been wonderful; as someone put it in almost biblical terms, 'he came amongst us.' Well, he did and it meant a huge amount to people that he'd bothered to come and that he spent time. Far longer than scheduled. He excels at this sort of thing. He enjoys meeting and talking to people and it shows.

★★★★★

This has been Thorney's week of limelight, the media circus has descended upon us and we've been much in the public eye, but a flood is a flood, nine houses under water although nobody's drowned and in fact the water's receded for the moment. So there's a slightly desperate sense of picking over the bones for something new to report. Rod and Hol who are conveniently close to dry land even had a visit from a German camera crew yesterday. There's a BBC van parked in the Drewell's drive with a camera on an extending arm to get overhead shots of the village. As I pass with the boat I overhear an interview with a woman who it turns out is not from round here and has only been visiting her friend, and no, she's fine and dry where she lives, thank you. A look of grim disappointment on the reporter's face. No drama, no drowning.

To add to the mêlée, BBC *Countryfile* came to Thorney yesterday afternoon. They'd been in touch over the weekend wanting to film Nick, then Rod and Holly, then me in our respective houses. I've no idea how they got my number. By late afternoon they phoned to say they were running behind schedule and had only just got to Rod. Wanting to go out for a run I splashed down the road to talk to them. Through the window I could see filming in progress and heard the familiar phrase I remember from when film crews came to the smokery and there'd be hours of retakes, '... Could we just do that scene again so that I can get more of you entering the room...' Roddy looked decidedly pissed off as he followed instructions and reversed back out of the room. I had no compunction in apologising that I'd run out of time and had to be getting on. They didn't seem in the slightest bit put out. In the event I don't think the piece is ever going to be used because much more important things are happening downriver.

★★★★★

This morning get out by boat and drive to the nearest post office. Martock road cut off, so headed to South Petherton instead. On the hill up to New Cross the road was like a river, streams pouring off the fields, the run-off so rapid now with the earth already waterlogged. It's all heading down into the river Parrett.

After lunch, useful site meeting between Ed Colegrave, our builder and Peter from the insurance company. We go through the house downstairs room by room detailing the damage and agreeing what needs to be done. Ed will now produce a costing and when that's approved things can start. Once we've dried out that is. And at the moment we're going backwards. The water is definitely coming back up, across the lawn now and just creeping up to the front door. Good thing they came today.

Ed will be back on Monday with his team so that they can see what to expect. I like him. He's got a firm handshake, looks you in the eye. And a nice smile. Son of a Devon farmer, he's a different breed of builder. Seems reliable.

Meanwhile I'm determined to have another go at fighting the flood to keep it out of the house.

Busy afternoon getting the pumps out, strategically positioned and then turned on. Seal up the doors again, screwing back the boarding and mastic round the edges. Just over a month since I was doing exactly the same. Inside I shut down the blowers and drying kit – peace again – and lift them onto chairs and tables out of the way of the water. I got the message when they were installed that these are very expensive pieces of kit. It's strange, I feel quite different this time round at the prospect of being flooded again, no sense of panic or dread. Defending the house is almost academic, a game; the worst has already happened, the damage done.

To supper up the road with Simon and Jayne and meet Michele and Terry Bradley, their neighbours. Their children were at primary school with ours'. They'd just been up to see their son who works in Soho in the film world. Terry says, 'When you're in London, no one ever looks at you. Everyone avoids your eyes.' An interesting observation from a country man. Their other son lives in Moorland down river, his house surrounded by flood water though they think he'll stay dry. Conversation turns to railways, Terry and Simon are real train buffs. Michele remembers using the local line from Somerton station as a child to get everywhere. Memories of a closer community, of the signalman who shot rabbits from the window of his hut, 'you'd see the wooden flap slowly raise and the barrel of the gun poking out, then crack' ; how she'd frequently forget her hat on the train and the station master would phone up her Mum, 'Mrs H, we've got Michele's hat again!' Everyone knew everyone, a root ball of connections that the railway enhanced. Before Beeching cut it all.

Back home to the pumps. They're going flat out but the water's creeping back into the house. Waders on and walk down river. The level right back up again, spilling over into the moor in all the usual places. I've noticed in their literature that the EA tend to describe this as 'overtopping' as if it was something carefully planned when in fact the river is freely pouring over a bank that's been allowed to subside for over fifteen years. All of it on its way back into our houses. It makes me furious because the buggers should be out here, boots on the ground, witnessing this so that they can do something about it but there's never a sign of them.

It's beautiful out here though. The wind has dropped for the moment, even some stars. A pair of swans like fighter aircraft, flying low overhead, necks outstretched, beat of wings, rasping the air, repositioning in the flood. And then from the village, the hoot of an owl.

Chapter Eight

HANGING ON

Water back into the main part of the house after just a week. Creeping into the kitchen again. Despite that, busy, satisfying day. Getting everything up off the ground. Tidying the clutter in the conservatory and upstairs.

Great excitement. Another text from Utta from down under. It's compressed, mainly consonants, hard to decipher but I'm pretty sure she's just arrived in Adelaide. I can almost feel the sun.

Tim Gray the electrician comes down to mend the immersion heater in the bathroom. Takes him just a couple of minutes, the safety switch had popped. Lucky that he was able to respond so quickly; living upstirs in a flooded house, with no proper heating and the loos not working, that hot bath is my one essential luxury.

James Crowden to lunch with Pauline Rook, Rod and Holly joined us. Pauline was the best photographer we ever used at the smokery. I remember her taking photos of racks of eel in the hot smoker. She had a Hasselblad camera that made a wonderful silky click–click as she fired the shutter. Most photographers spent hours setting up their lighting but she was all done in about five minutes and produced some of

*best images we ever had. She's a lovely lady, quietly spoken,
eyes watchful for the possible photo. Like a blackbird for the
worm. They hope to bring an old friend, a consultant to the
Drainage Board, to look at the river bank and the flooding
here. Meanwhile James brings more generous pies to go with
the soup.*

Pumps are still going bravely but I switch them off in the late
afternoon, reluctantly, but as the saying goes, 'No use farting
against thunder'. The floodwater is rising with a vengeance,
three inches in the main and nine in the old part of the house.
Another session of clearing upstairs. It's like a giant jig-saw or
cross-word puzzle; addictive but can't do it for too long, I run
out of steam or get distracted. When I return to it refreshed,
often see a solution to the log-jam. Bizarre and rather pathetic
that life has come down to this but it lends purpose. I feel I've
achieved something.

When I'm working in the rooms up here I have the
radio on – Radio 4 – for company and for its many good
programmes. It's the great advantage of radio that you're free
to roam, work wherever you want, not pinned to a screen.
And as my radio is old and gets Long Wave, it also gets the
Test Match cricket. In the summer I'll have it beside me as
I work in the veg patch listening to the commentary. I was
never a cricketer, only played it at a very junior level but it
is one of those sports that can captivate the listener and you
don't have to have played. My great aunt loved cricket and was
very knowledgeable. My father loved his cricket too. In my
memory of childhood summers long ago I have a picture of
Dad, a picnic on Dartmoor, leaning over the radio, absorbed,
listening to the slow, rich descriptive commentary of John
Arlott, the Voice of Cricket, who could one moment evoke
the terrifying pace and menace of the West Indian fast bowling
and the next describe, 'The trees away in the distance heaving
under the wind.' With Arlott you always felt you were there
at the ground.

To supper with Margaret and John in Stembridge, a couple of miles south. They've been very kind, this is about my third visit. Margie takes my bundle of washing from me and bungs it straight into the machine. From their house I run over One Tree hill to the start of the flood on the Hambridge road. It's beautiful, eerily quiet, no traffic. A feeling that the lanes and the farmhouses have been abandoned, just the lap of water as I hit the flood and turn back. A hot shower and lovely supper. Talk about their childhood, how John's father was killed in Italy during the war, buried at Assisi; how important his grandparents were to him. They were the salt of the earth, John spent huge amounts of time with his grandfather, a gardener, following him around and helping him.

Home and another productive spell of sorting the rooms. And so to bed with Leigh Fermor's biography. I'm following him as he walks across Europe as a young man in the 1930s heading to the Black Sea and Constantinople which he was later to describe in two wonderful books, *A Time for Gifts* and *Between Woods and Water*. Fall asleep as he is making his way through Germany.

SATURDAY FEBRUARY 9TH

News just coming in of serious flooding downriver in the village of Moorland above Bridgwater. The moors around the village have been flooded since just after New Year but this last week, on the 5th, the same night as the storms battered the coast, the water level rose dramatically and in the early hours of Friday 7th police helicopters were hovering overhead with loudspeakers advising villagers to evacuate their homes. Must have been terrifying especially for the children and the oldies. The water waist-deep and in most cases nowhere for them to go except to emergency reception centres as many of the houses are single storey. Here, we've been able to live upstairs and we're only a short wade from dry land; down there flooding is on another scale altogether. Emergency calls have also been put out to help evacuate some hundreds of cattle. Mike Curtis from Thorney made two trips yesterday with his tractor and cattle trailer to a farmer, James Winslade, just outside Moorland to pick up two lots, twenty animals a time that will be housed on a farm near here. It's about fourteen miles each way and Mike said he was staggered by the amount of water below Burrowbridge as he approached Moorland. Flood water stretched for what seemed like miles in all directions. Worse than here.

Listening on the news to interviews with villagers in Moorland, hearing their stories, their shock, distress and emotion is like reliving our own experience five weeks ago. There's also huge anger at the way the whole thing was handled, the lack of warning, being woken by the searchlight in the night and the voice of the loudspeaker from the police helicopter overhead. Someone said, 'That was a prime example of how not to carry out an evacuation. It was chaotic, no checking of who was left or where people had gone.' As people emerge from the initial shock, I sense they're beginning to wonder also where the water came from so suddenly: apparently in the early hours of the morning it rose by nearly a metre in a few minutes. There are deep suspicions that somewhere sluices were raised to save parts of Taunton or Bridgwater. My own feeling is that it was the result of the heavy rain on the hills all round reaching ground already flooded. A bit like a tidal wave. In the event nearly a hundred and twenty homes have been flooded.

It is at times like these, when a major incident has been declared, that the Gold Silver Bronze command structure should kick in to deal with the situation. The concept was created by the Metropolitan Police in October 1985 following the Broadwater Farm riot in north London when Police constable Keith Blakelock was murdered. It was realised that the usual rank-based command didn't work for such sudden events: it had never been clear who was actually in operational charge of the police during the riot. The new structure separates strategic command (gold) from tactical (silver) from operational (bronze) with the aim of putting the most appropriate person in the right position at the right time. Normally it works well, but this flood is an extraordinary event, a huge, probing, shifting enemy – not dissimilar to a huge forest fire, wind-driven, in Australia or the States. Very hard to predict and control. In the eyes of the locals things have not been handled at all well. It seems there's been a distinct lack of briefing at operational level and a lack of coordination.

The Moorland situation is far worse than we experienced but at least the world knows it's happening and the emergency services, police, Marines, volunteers, they're all there working flat-out. The EA is pumping for all its worth: across the area over a hundred pumps are going full blast, in addition to the 19 Dutch pumps just bought in from Holland, adding 50% more capacity. It's become the largest-ever mobile pumping operation in the UK. A command structure is in place though evidently not functioning as well as it might. By contrast when the flood hit Thorney and surrounding areas at the beginning of January there was no help, no sign of a pump, no one knew about us. The focus was on the stranded island of Muchelney. We felt totally abandoned by the EA and that made us all very angry. Not until Martin Hesp put us on the map with his piece in the Western Morning News. Meanwhile still nothing's happened, no pumping, and we've all been sitting in floodwater – barring a few days respite – for well over five weeks. We shall be pickled soon.

★★★★★

James Winslade's story is exceptional because it highlights the desperate plight of man and animals trapped in the flood as well as the extraordinary mutual support that farming communities display in times of need.

James who farms near Moorland is also the area representative for the Inland Drainage Board and had been pressing the EA to run the pumps since Northmoor first started to flood after Christmas. If they could get the water away, they could be ahead of the game. But no, they can't do anything over Christmas and the New Year. Eventually they agree to run the two electric pumps at Northmoor pumping station and more are brought in as the flooding worsens. Now it is the beginning of February and things are getting desperate. Over the road from his house is a post with the height of last year's flood marked on it. The water is already up to the mark and rising. In the barns across the yard he has 550 cattle in danger of drowning. There is no way he can get them out on his own. It's a Herculean task.

On Wednesday, February 5th, the day after meeting Prince Charles on the top of Burrow Mump, the landmark hill nearby, the Emergency services are trying to persuade him to stay. They promise to erect a protective ring bank around the farm. By that afternoon, however, as no one has appeared, he decides to evacuate. As a last resort with the new phone he was given at Christmas he decides to put out a call on Twitter and Facebook, a cry for help. The response is overwhelming and immediate. Tractors and trailers – like Mike Curtis's – start arriving from all around. It's a massive operation. Having loaded the cattle, they can't take the road down to Moorland, it's impassable, the water in the village five feet deep. They have to turn up to Burrowbridge. James has marked the road with cattle stakes, like poles in the snow. Even so a truck slides off the road into the ditch and temporarily blocks the way. Two other tractors are lost. It's not long before the A361 at Burrowbridge is also under water, too deep for the lorries which are meeting them there. Instead they take the old route down the river bank, accessible half-way to Burrowbridge, which skirts the flood water and Moorland village using the bank as a causeway. It's the best route but it is treacherous for big vehicles. Unpaved, muddy, slippery. An old badger sett dug deep into the bank itself has blown, allowing the river to pour through and, though now repaired, is another hazard.

James loads cattle onto the rescue trailers all day Wednesday, all Thursday till late in the night and finally through to Friday midday. For three days and nights he hardly sleeps. If not taken straight to their new hosts, the cattle go to Sedgemoor market in Bridgwater, there to be confronted by officialdom. 'We can't have them here.' COBRA however overrules: all cattle must be got out, they'll sort the red tape. Eventually all his animals are safe, dispersed to some nine farms in a forty mile radius. When they start the evacuation on the Wednesday the water is up to the toe of his boot, when they finish on the Friday it is above his waist, a rise of one and a half metres. There are other farmers too who need help evacuating cattle. His neighbour Geoff Miller has 300 head that are also taken out on the Friday. In the end James and his neighbours manage to move some 1500 sheep, 1200 cattle and 120 horses.

Evacuation complete, shutting down his house and farm and his parent's home nearby he encounters one of the most poignant images of the whole episode. On the wall outside their house, he meets a hare, surrounded by water, stiff with fear. He can't reach it to save it. 'I'll always wonder what happened to it.'

Finding a home for his 550 head of cattle is just part of the problem; providing feed for them is another. To reduce the numbers 160 head are sold immediately. Meanwhile each of the farms looking after his cattle agree to do the feeding but James needs to supply the fodder. His own fodder is on his farm surrounded by flood and is irretrievable. Again he puts out a call on Twitter. Again the response is overwhelming: 197 calls and offers of help on the first day alone. Twenty lorries a day for nearly two months roll in from all over the country, some as far away as Scotland. It's the biggest movement of silage and fodder ever known from one call. Tesco's are brilliant and agree to offer nearly half a million pounds-worth of haulage as well as the services of their logistics officer. A spoke and hub system is devised. Farmers in other parts of the country are able to deliver fodder to designated collection sites nearest to them where they load during the day onto trailers hired from Eddie Stobart which are then hitched onto distribution trucks after they've completed their daily deliveries. They reach Somerset in waves at 10pm, 12pm and 3am. It's like a military operation.

When the fodder arrives at Sedgemoor market it still has to be distributed to all the farms throughout the county that are hosting animals – and there are many beside James's – displaced by the flood. Help pours in, generous and timely. The NFU is much involved, so too voluntary organisations like the Farming Community Network who assess the various needs of the farms for their stock they're holding. Another charity helps fund distribution costs. Local farm groups loan machinery, kit, loaders, trailers, JCB Fast Tracks; feed mills provide food for calves. Young Farmers and volunteers give their time. James's wife works every hour alongside him in this huge distribution challenge.

At the same time the public are following the story on TV and radio. Hundreds of letters, small gifts, and offerings pour in, 'To the farmer I've just seen on the telly, here's £5 to help you' or the woman from Chepstow who says she can't help with the animals but she can bake cakes and arrives with a car full of them.

What is remarkable is the support that farmers, the world over, are prepared to give each other at the drop of a hat, more than in any other industry. It's probably because they already form a tight-knit community amongst themselves but it perhaps also goes back to the time when they helped each other with harvests, threshing, moving animals, gathering in crops when extra labour was needed – as they still do at times. James Winslade thinks it's more because 'we're at the bottom of the pile so we have to stick together'. Whatever the reasons, their resilience and self-reliance is impressive as is their innate initiative which comes from having to cope on their own. The unfolding of these floods has shown that in times of emergency they provide a vital first response, the ones most quickly able to get things going again. Certainly around here we saw first-hand with the Thorney tractor ferry service that they were far more effective than any of the local authorities.

*****

Wade down to Muchelney for lunch with Ingrid and David, just back from visiting their son, Will, in Western Australia. Very windy by the gaps in the hedges with short choppy waves but wild and beautiful and a touch of danger and adrenaline. Talk to myself as I gently roll-walk. It's snug and dry in the waders, in the floodwater, like being in your own small boat. And self-contained. The chest flap pocket carries essentials, mobile phone, cash and keys. I've had several phone calls while in deep floodwater, one two days ago from a coffee shop in Melbourne from a very good friend ringing to see how we were.

Once on dry land in the village there's another mile at least to their house, so David picks me up. Once out of the habitat for which they're designed, waders are horribly uncomfortable. As useless as boats on dry land. Great welcome from Ing and David. We've know them almost as long as we've been in Somerset, nearly forty years. Peter and Liz Nightingale also present. Liz hands me a bag of home cooked ready-meals which some kind person has been bringing to the church. Ingrid also gives me the remains of the fabulous lamb and rice salad we had for lunch. Very grateful to them. Wade home like a smuggler, rucksack bulging with goodies.

Rod and Holly also flooded again. Roddy tells me they're both feeling pretty low. It all seems never-ending. And work so difficult for them, both their workshops under water. Very tough.

*****

Back home, water in the house still rising. The wind too as the storm gathers strength. Putting more weights on the shed roof and lashing it down with a hairnet of ropes as they do on the croft roofs in the north of Scotland, each end weighted down by several concrete blocks. Busy too with the upstairs junkyard. Thank god for the skip that arrived yesterday. It's huge, big as a battle tank sitting square on the drive. Managed to tip in all the old carpet and flooring, also the fridges, dishwasher and sofas. Very sad to get rid of the big sofa but it had been ruined by the floodwater. Enjoy the challenge of doing it all on my own with minimal lifting, using a ladder and plank as a shallow ramp to push the items up and over the edge. Disconcerting how quickly it fills. Get inside and do lots of rearranging to make space. From the cupboards in Oliver's room upstairs, I tip boxes of old school books, notes and files creating lovely new space that I can now use to stow some of the flood jumble.

★★★★★

We've had no paper delivery for weeks now but I pick up the odd one when I'm shopping, so I have one today. I finally settle to read it with my supper on the bathroom floor. In the section of world news is a piece on Aleppo, Syria, with an image that stops me in my tracks.

It's a picture of a father with his three boys just after their home has been hit by an airstrike from Assad regime fighter jets. They are sitting in a pathetic row on the steps of a building. The father is holding his baby, his eyes fixed worriedly on the little face, his hand cradling its head. The baby's hand is stretched out touching his father's chest as if for reassurance. On one side of him a son of about eight years old, in jeans far too big for him, eyes closed, his mouth wide open, cries, distraught. At this moment he is uncomforted, alone. In his hand a small twist of paper, perhaps something he was eating before the bomb fell. On the other side the eldest boy, perhaps sixteen, looks across at his baby brother in his father's arms, but he is dazed, in a trance. And though he looks, he does not see. Their hair, their shoes, their clothes are covered in white dust from the explosion. There is no sign of the mother – if she's still alive. It's a scene of utter human desolation. A still-life in the futility of war and its effect on innocent victims.

I can't help wondering, 'What will happen to them all

and what lives are in prospect for the boys?' The two youngest are the about the same age as our grandchildren.

It's an image that puts into immediate perspective all our woes and grumbles about the flooding; so puny and trifling by contrast. We have so much and they have absolutely nothing.

The desperate state of their country calls to mind the first lines of WB Yeats's poem *The Second Coming* written in 1919:

'Turning and turning in the widening gyre
The falcon cannot hear the falconer;
Things fall apart; the centre cannot hold
Mere anarchy is loosed upon the world
The blood-dimmed tide is loosed, and everywhere
The ceremony of innocence is drowned;
The best lack all conviction, whilst the worst
Are full of passionate intensity.'

MONDAY FEBRUARY 10TH

Couldn't resist walking down river bank last night. Light just going. Stunning out there. Huge inland sea. Cold wind. Ice-clear and moon half full. The big line of poplars sketched against the sky. Calls of innumerable wildfowl. At the pumping station none of the pumps working but then there's nowhere to pump, the river is brim full.

On the news last night, heavy flooding on the Thames in Berkshire, Henley down to Chertsey. Some very unhappy people. Lots of anger, people wanting to kick out at the authorities; that need to blame someone, to find a scapegoat. Like listening to ourselves at the beginning. In many cases their flood has been and gone.

Sparkling day. Another glorious break before another storm rolls in. A fleeting visit from Hol in the morning, like a bird alighting. 'Just checking you're all right'. She's troubled and restless, she cannot get to her work as it's either flooded in the jewellery workshop or scattered about the house. To be able to work would be so helpful, healing.

Late afternoon and the building team arrives. Ed calls on his mobile from the edge of the flood. I wade up to collect them with the boat, bringing them back to the house in two groups. Like the D-day landings. All the trades there, carpenter, electrician, plumber, plasterer, decorator. And a kitchen designer, a pretty lady, with lovely eyes and smile. I'm not sure they would have come if it had just been a normal job but there is perhaps an element of excitement and curiosity to cross the flood and see inside a flooded house. A good start, they can't do anything but it gives them a chance to eyeball what has to be done and what to order. Ed had warned them all they'd need wellies. They slosh about making notes. The theme, I tell them, is planning for the future, living *with* the flood, so everything raised wherever possible. As soon as the water recedes and we dry out, they'll all be back to start work. I'm impressed by Ed's ability to have got them all here on time and together today. They're all self-employed, work for him only when needed as sub-contractors. Obviously has a good relationship with them.

A short wade down the road to supper with Chris and Rita. Roast vegetables with chicken and chorizo. Lots of wine. She's such a good cook. Chris recalls when he first started work and earning, 'The proudest moment of my life was when I bought a washing machine for my mum because hers had died.' This was when she was on her own, bringing up a large family on very little. It's been so good getting to know them better. They've been very kind to me.

Another rat encounter tonight, a scurrying shape in the sitting room as I pass on my way upstairs, smaller than Mr Big but unwelcome nonetheless. However after much bashing around, no sign of him and at least Glen's new door is now firmly fixed across the stairs on the half landing to stop him coming up. Sit wrapped in rugs in the bedroom in front of Paxman's programme on the First World War which I've been looking forward to but sadly nod off and only catch the credits at the end. Long chat on the phone with Emily afterwards.

And so to bed. Drift off to the boom of the mill upstream. River very high.

WEDNESDAY FEBRUARY 12TH

A good day yesterday. Shopped in Langport. The great metropolis! Stocked up on goodies and wine for thank yous. Getting out, the usual major event to organise: packing shoes, wellies, carrier bags, remembering keys for the car and the house. As I was mid-wade, heard from Ed, the builder, and from Peter the Insurance, the costings have been agreed so inching forward.

Rod and Holly popped in for tea. H. in much better form. We are all tense, bracing ourselves for the big storm forecast later today and the rain that'll come with it.

More news of the Thames valley flooding. Listening to elderly people in Chertsey in the aftermath of their experiences last night. They have that dazed look. There is less of the anger shown by house owners interviewed last night, more confused, soft clucking noises like chickens still in shock after a visit from the fox.

Wind beginning to howl outside. I was on the phone to someone after supper in the bathroom and heard myself saying, 'I'm worried about the shed roof', and almost as I uttered the words I heard a slithering overhead as a tile detached itself. A horrible sound, quite unnerving as if the storm is trying to prise the house apart. I was genuinely able to add, 'But I'm even more worried about the house.'

★★★★★

This morning, water rising. Eight inches back in the house.

From the upstairs window I've noticed every morning early, rain or shine, regular as clockwork, before the passenger service starts, a small tractor passes, it's rather battered and elderly, and chugs past the house pushing through the flood.

It belongs to Den in one of the council houses beyond John Leach's pottery. He has ground beyond Kingsbury and horses to feed. Sometimes he has a box on the back. I am amazed that he isn't swamped, the water often well up to the belly of the tractor engine but he always gets through and back again in the evening. I've not yet met him to talk to but there's always a friendly wave. I admire his independence and dogged determination to brave the flood each day.

Soon after Den comes the tractor ferry, still carrying people daily to and from work; the service is now in its sixth week. Over that time we've got to recognise the passengers, know who's on the early run and who's back late. Since a national emergency was declared at the end of January, however, there are many more vehicles involved now. Land Rovers and 4x4's owned by volunteers, some coming from miles away to offer their services ferrying people through the flood during the day time. Fire Service trucks have also appeared, they're enormous but actually only able to take three or four passengers at the most. The trouble is that each vehicle that passes creates a great bow wave that barrels down the road battering and ricocheting off the walls either side. It has already destroyed a brick wall at the far end of the road. Our garden wall is beginning to suffer badly. Several stones shifted after the last flood. I'm beginning to wonder how long it can withstand this constant thumping.

It's a lovely old wall built of blue lias stone, wide and deep and probably as old as the house, held together by ageing wheezy mortar. In its dotage it harbours a whole natural world of its own amidst a labyrinth of holes and tunnels. More a living bank than a wall. Plants, amongst them stonecrop, a tiny succulent with bright yellow flowers you'd think belonged only in the Karoo desert grow on top while purple aubrieta festoons the sides in spring. Birds nest in its crevices, robins and blue tits especially. Mice sidle in and out of its hidden passageways, busy foraging, even the odd weasel I've seen, while fat snails hide from the thrush. As I work in the veggie garden over spring and summer, passing neighbours and walkers lean on its broad shelf and chat over the top. We love this wall and feel very protective of it as it takes the impact of wave after wave from passing traffic. Richard England is the best driver, he passes very slowly with the tractor and his bow wave is minimal. It's the newcomers to the area who are the worst. Unsure of the depth of water and inexperienced, they charge at the flood creating waves three feet high which reverberate through the garden, even into the house. The apples love it as it propels them further into our garden and nearer the house which they're longing to explore. If you're passing in waders you can be swamped or carried away; we've all worked out there is only one thing to do and that's to take up a position in the middle of the road and force them to slow down. If I'm in the house or garden I've taken to bellowing at them, 'SLOW DOWN' like some demented old bugger. It must sound most ungrateful to the volunteer drivers who've come from far afield to offer their services.

★★★★★

I've arranged to take the rocking chair for repair. I load it gently into the boat along with the wheelbarrow. Once through the flood, I wheel it the half mile down the road to Luke, the carpenter I met in the crowd waiting for HRH. His workshop is very neat. He flooded too but he showed me a device he'd made that enabled him to raise his machinery: a steel plate, attached to the foot of an oak post, it slides under the object to be lifted and you can then either lever it up onto blocks or place a jack under the projecting heel fixed to the reverse side of the post. Using a car jack to lift heavy pieces of furniture or machinery is great but usually there's no room to get them under the furniture unless it's on legs. You need a good 8-10 inches working space. This tool is brilliant. I order one on the spot – for the future. Luke learnt his trade as a boat builder before becoming a traditional carpenter. To keep warm in his workshop he wears a wool hat with pigtails and looks just like Asterix – well, he is half French.

12.55AM FEBRUARY 12TH

View from the upstairs window. It's pissing with rain. Big storm, some of the worst weather we've seen. Boat, tethered on the lawn, spins round and round tugging at the anchor post. Armageddon. Roddy says it's up three inches in their house. Noticed earlier, their canoe is full of water, hardly used in recent weeks. No play now. Grim times. Gone on long enough. How much longer before it all ends? Wind outside roaring like a great engine. No jackdaws on Nick's roof today.

The storm passes around 2-ish yesterday afternoon followed by a much brighter day, with winds slowly dying. This seems to be the pattern: wind and storm followed on quickly by clear bright weather, until the next storm. Days of dark and light. Ten inches of water in the house now.

Tonight a good run. Willed myself to go, all the hassle of changing from wellies to waders to runners and back again but as soon as I was out there I loved it. Great feeling of liberation. Nearly a full moon sailing through clouds like a galleon in heavy seas.

Road deserted as I ran out through Kingsbury to Burrow Hill. This is one of the good things about the flood: the empty roads. Heard recently that over the river in Thorney South, caught between two floods, there is no traffic at all and the children have taken over the road to play. Happy as mud larks. Like the good old days. Back to hot bath and shepherd's pie, donated to the flood victims by some kind person. It's had quite a journey, but delicious.

Read on the bathroom floor, between phone calls from family and friends. One from cousins in Australia. Much enjoying Artemis Cooper's biography of Patrick Leigh Fermor. Colder outside but warm thanks to the gas heater lent by Tony up the road.

Tomorrow, off to London to collect Utta. Will stay the night with Oliver and Angelina and the boys. Very excited about seeing her; there've been no lengthy phone calls, just the odd text to make sure all's well. We'll drive home via Oxford to see Emily whose birthday is on Friday.

SATURDAY FEBRUARY 15TH

Lovely night with Ollie and family in London. In-between reading the boys their bedtime story, ask the eldest, aged six, how he is getting on with his new teacher in school. 'Oh very well,' he replies matter of factly, 'Mr Wright says me and Omah are the most wise.' Well, that's reassuring.

Utta arrived at the house early, having been dropped miles away by a grumpy taxi. She seems remarkably perky and full of beans after the flight. We take the two older boys to school then chat over innumerable cups of tea with Angelina. Much playing with the youngest; he is very solid, when you lift him up it's a bit like holding a sand bag. A damp one.

Up to Oxford through driving rain. In the car, tales of Utta's trip, vivid images, people and places we know, heat, and the smells of Australia; outside, grey, grim landscape of swollen rivers, the Thames sprawled half across Oxford, flooded fields, and endless sheets of rain. We meet Emily at her local restaurant. She is just back from an overseas trip. A meal of travellers' tales, interwoven with news from the home front and life in a flooded house. That night, a growing storm, buffeting her house. I sleep badly, envisaging all the damage being done at home, the shed being blown away. Tiles being ripped off the roof of our house. I feel terrible that I'm not there to defend it. I shall phone Roddy in the morning to check. Meanwhile outside Emily's house car alarms are going off. Go out in the middle of the night to inspect, thinking it might be ours. The wind is howling. Just now and then, glimpses of a full moon between shredded clouds. The wildest night. The fury of the storm actually frightening.

We are home now. I remembered to pack Utta's waders which is good because the water is as deep in the house and garden as it was when she left three weeks ago. But, great relief, everything is intact. The shed still there. Roof still on the house. Great mats of weed torn from the moor float half submerged in the road and in the garden. But what a grim welcome home for Utta: she left in the flood and she's back to the flood. The house more cold and lifeless than ever.

SUNDAY FEBRUARY 16TH

Sparkling day in the wake of the storms. The sky washed clear. The gulls have descended, raucous and squabbling, around the edges of the field over the river.

Today James Crowden and Pauline Rook are bringing Dan Alsop, a friend and former chartered engineer with the Inland Drainage Board, to look at the river bank and the flood and give us his thoughts on what measures we might take to protect ourselves in the future. Roddy joins us as we make our way down river. I can see Dan with his professional eye quietly taking it all in as we walk beside him rather like dogs yapping around his feet, pointing out various features that we are particularly aerated about, vehemently expressing views on what we see as contributory causes to our flooding: the bank subsidence, the pumps that never seem to be turned on, and the part played by the Isle flowing into the moor. I've often found when speaking to someone with real experience and authority on a subject that the solution to a problem that seemed so simple and straightforward in my own mind, all of a sudden seems much more complicated. All certainty starts to dissolve.

Dan politely acknowledges the points we raise but in such a way that seems to take the steam out of them. Yes, the bank has certainly subsided and every effort should be made to repair it but the damaged length is too short to have made a significant difference to the flood. And there is no give on the question of pumping, the basic premise remains: our pump won't operate until 'overtopping' ceases at the Parrett spillway into Aller moor or the Tone spillways into Curry Moor. It's all rather sobering and I feel like a bottle of fizzy water that's been opened too long. And dejected. However on the way back, things improve. He spots the low bank to the old catch water ditch running at right angles to the river behind the Temperley's house. If this were beefed up, raised and reinforced, it could provide proper flood protection for the village. With small prospect of reducing the flooding on the moor, he recommends it would be much better to concentrate our efforts on really good defence – 'a ring bank and pumping station', if the funds can be found – he adds somewhat ominously.

It is the best advice we've had. The possibility of doing something along these lines has already been muted by several of us in the village but this is its first professional endorsement. Certainly one to discuss when we have our first meeting.

★★★★★

It is very good to have Utta back. My best friend home again. It's been positive for each of us, too, to be on our own, all the while knowing that we'll soon be back together again. It refreshes and revitalises us. Over the ensuing days we talk and talk, catching up not just on the main events that occurred for each of us during our time apart but the little things, the details, nuances, that make up the bits in between. Often the most important. Like the mortar between the blocks.

After a separation, though, there is always a period of time needed to synchronise your lives again, readjusting from being each one of us on our own to being a couple together. From Solo to Duo. On your own you have only yourself to think of, you develop ways of doing things that won't work when you're together. Little things like getting up early: I simply turn on the light to make my way across the bedroom to the bathroom next door. Now that Utta is home, I'm back to creeping around in the dark, tripping over my shoes, fumbling for the latch to open the door as quietly as possible so as not to wake her.

I remember back in my elver days a fishermen, one of the old guard, once recalling as we chatted one night after he'd weighed in,

'I like it when the missus is out skittlin cos I kin cut me toenails on the kitchen vloor.'

Looking back to the 1950s, my father was often away for long periods, over a year on one occasion. Companies didn't help to bring families together then as they do now. For servicemen down the ages it has always been part of the life, those long separations, months, years at a time from families back home, often in dangerous places. One of the most poignant accounts of this is in N.A.M Rodger's book, *Command of the Ocean*, in which he writes:

'Separation had always been one of the hardships of the sea service, and was particularly hard in the blockade years … Admiral Collingwood complained that 'my family are actually strangers to me.' When he died in 1810 he had not seen his wife and daughters since the outbreak of war seven years before, nor the garden he loved so much. In one of his letters he had written home, 'Tell me how do the trees which I planted thrive? Is there shade under the three oaks for a comfortable summer seat? Do the poplars grow at the walk, and does the wall of the terrace stand firm?'

TUESDAY FEBRUARY 18TH

Rained all day yesterday, with odd brighter spells. A dark grey day where it seemed perfectly permissible to sit upstairs and read and chat. Utta full of cluck and buzz about the plans for the new kitchen, very excited about it. Like a chook with a worm. We had lunch by the window in our bedroom. She's delighted with the rocking chair now restored by Luke – it's got its rock back. Was thinking of leaving it with him till her birthday but couldn't think how to wrap it. In between rain, lovely light outside and reflections on the ceiling. We have delicious cake for pud, the one given to me by the cousins at Angela's funeral.

Ran down to the pumping station last night. None of

them working but hardly surprising. The level of flood on the moor is now as high as it has ever been and in places spilling over into the river – first time I've ever seen it do this. Only a thin path between the two bodies of water. Foul slithery running but loved it nonetheless. Heard the owl again.

★★★★★

Our woodpile is growing. Strewn along the edge of the flood all the way down river along the high water mark is the flotsam and jetsam of the past seven weeks. Every time we go out we gather it by the armful. Sawn logs from apple trees cut the other side of the moor, branches of willow and poplar, twisted and hoary roots of thorn, hard as iron, pieces of fencing, planks weathered silver grey by the wind and the water and piles of sticks, perfect for kindling. We stack them upright around an old tree at the end of the garden, wigwam style so that they can dry and where they form a cascade of colour and shapes, growing and changing all the time as we add more each day. We shall be warm this coming winter. A small compensation from nature. And, as they used to say, the wood will warm us twice: once from the cutting and carrying, once from the burning in the grate.

I'm increasingly aware of morale and spirits beginning to droop. Signs of stress. Faces tired and drawn. The endless flog to get to work, the struggle into waders even to go downstairs. It's gone on long enough, we've had it to the back teeth. Even the flood itself seems tired. It is huge, sullen, oily grey-brown; it just sits there like some uninvited guest. It's beginning to hide all sorts of rubbish, mats of reed, drowned logs, household objects, floating gas bottles that bump into your legs as you wade down the road. I wouldn't be surprised if there was even the odd body. Like a scene from the end of the world. The waves of bobbing apples that besieged the house when it all started back in January have lost their perkiness, most of them vanished, only the odd rotting fruit now skulking like thugs at a crime scene.

There seems to be only one winner in all of this: our leeks in the veg patch have taken on new life, they're enormous, as big as cricket stumps. Not quite sure what they'll taste like.

Chapter Nine

DRYING OUT

Out of curiosity I've been looking at the story of the Flood
in the King James's Bible. I learn that it is a story echoed in
the literature of many other religions, including the Quran; a
story of punishment and purification, about wiping the slate
clean and starting afresh. When I look at the text, though,
where God in his wrath says, 'I will destroy man whom I
have created', there is a suggestion later that He feels he has
overreacted, been too harsh, for when the flood recedes, the
narrative continues,' And the Lord said in his heart, I will not
again curse the ground any more for man's sake…neither will I
again smite any more every thing living, as I have done.' After
the great purging a sense of peace seems to return. A wish to
get on with normal life again.

We would welcome that too.

*Both woke early this morning for some reason and lay in the
dark enjoying a cuppa. Almost pitch black till around 6am
then very rapidly light filled the sky and we could see the
outlines of the trees and the orchard. Then through the open
bedroom window we hear the dawn chorus of garden birds, the*

blackbird amongst them. We lie there listening. It fills us with hope that spring is round the corner.

Definite signs of change. The gale force winds have gone, the jet stream, locked in position for weeks, has veered away; weather forecasts are all of a sudden less doom laden. The flood water in the house, eighteen inches at the deepest point, is now falling back.

The sun is out. Surely this must be the end of it. Sure that Noah, peering from his upper deck, would have felt the same. Shame we couldn't have met for a chat, compared notes.

Walk together down the river bank. In the main channel behind the pumping station, a pair of swans, catching the breeze with wings cupped like sails. When they stop to feed, both tipping over in time together, tail feathers in the air, it's like watching synchronised swimmers.

Meanwhile there is a growing pressure to think ahead and to make decisions. We know that when the house has dried out the builders will be in and wanting to get to work without delay. We have to have a clear idea of what we want and have it ordered, ready to install. We start with the kitchen. At its heart is the old Rayburn which we've had for over twenty years. It was second hand and quite elderly when we bought it. It could take several hours of coaxing and negotiation before you could fry an egg on top but it has been wonderful for slow cooking, stews, soups – nothing too strenuous. Over the years like an ageing alcoholic it has become increasingly fond of central heating oil, glugging its way through at least 40 litres a week but we have forgiven all that because like an old friend, it has always been there, always welcoming. Dogs have slept by it, clothes dried on it; it has been the warm heart of the house. The boiler man says he could probably get it going again, 'Tis only a glorified paraffin heater inside a bliddy great carcass. Nothing complicated like.' But we've noticed it's begun to be incontinent, leaking paraffin onto the kitchen floor from the thin copper tube that feeds it from outside. Prostate trouble perhaps. And that was before the flood which has left a rusty mark nearly half way up the oven door. Like standing round the sick bed of an elderly friend, we have whispered conversations so that it can't hear us discussing its future. Now is the time to replace it. Remember what the insurance people said: new for old, like for like.

There is an Aga showroom not far from us. We decide to have a day out stopping en route in the little market town of Ilminster to browse and for lunch. The showroom, when we get there, is an impressive building, full of beautiful kitchens, pine tables and units positioned round cookers, mostly Agas big as ship's boilers, all eye-wateringly expensive. The vision of rural life, the country look. Lots of prospective customers in lodden coats, tweed, and country hats. It all feels a bit stiff and smug, but lovely kit. We like the look of an electric one – an Everhot made by a different company. Very solid and well machined, the oven doors are magnetic and close like a kiss. We leave, clutching sheaves of literature for study back home.

★★★★★

Another day of sorting and getting rid of 'stuff' while the skip is here. Amongst the flotsam and jetsam piled on the beds upstairs are boxes of old photos tucked in their wallets. I've decided I'm going to go through them and keep only the very best but it doesn't work; within minutes I'm lost in the past. The oldest photos, like leaves in a pond, lie at the bottom. They were taken in Aix-en-Provence in the south of France during a year spent there in 1966/7 as part of my degree.

'Where would be a good place to go?' I had asked my tutor.

'Well, if you like the sun, the smell of pines, the sound of cicadas, then I think you'd like Aix.' He'd obviously had a great time there.

Few students took time off before university in those days. To be sent to study the language for a year on a grant, to be free in this beautiful old town, Cezanne's birthplace, was an extraordinary privilege. It was one of the best years of my life. I made lifelong friends, encountering new experiences, mixing with students of so many different nationalities: I remember going skiing once, (4 francs a night in a converted shepherd's hut) ten of us, from nine different countries, all speaking French. As a university town it thronged with young people throughout its narrow streets and leafy markets, its quiet squares and down its central avenue, the Cours Mirabeau, under the thick shade of the plane trees, where beautiful girls and their admirers sat in pavement cafes.

Yet it wasn't all beautiful and sun. In the winter the mistral blew, an icy wind down from the Alps and the town hunched against the cold. Those first few months were lonely at times too, especially when the French students vanished home for the weekend.

Then quite by chance I met a remarkable woman by the name of Mme Tailleux, a wonderful eccentric, who touched and enriched the loves of many who swam into her orbit. As I did one wintry afternoon on the doorstep of her old farmhouse in a small village outside Aix. Given her address by a friend, I was warmly greeted, and invited in for tea. Typical of her hospitality and total disregard for time, I ended up staying several days. Eileen Tailleux was from an affluent English family, educated by governesses between the wars, she spoke fluent French, was passionate about a myriad of causes, mostly in defence of the underdog. She must have been stunning as a young woman. Married to a French painter, Francis Tailleux, they'd bought a mas, a Provencal farmhouse, where she'd lived ever since. She had a wide range of literary and artistic friends, writers, painters, musicians and potters. She read voraciously, often well into the night, devouring the Le Monde newspaper, her glasses, usually with one stalk missing, balanced precariously on the bridge of her nose.

She had such energy. She loved the company of young people, loved conversation, discussion; meals round her table were an endless delight. I'm holding a photo now: the terrace of her house shaded from the sun, a group of us, all fellow students, having lunch around a long table with her at the head. In the distance you can just make out the hills blurred in the heat rising to the Mont Sainte-Victoire. I can almost smell the thyme, hear the pulse of the cicadas, the laughter and the voices. Three of those in the scene are still some of my closest friends. For all of us she opened our eyes to so many things, to different ways of thinking. We all loved her. By the time I met Eileen she'd long been separated, her children grown up. She was probably then in her late fifties, long hair, silver now, always wrapped in a scarf or cloth and still with the most wonderful blue eyes. I look back at her as a kind of Miss Jean Brodie, with her zest for life, her championing of causes. Youth, vitality, curiosity were god-given in her eyes and she was hard on those she considered idlers, parasites.

She was also wonderfully eccentric, a one-off. A fabulous cook but her kitchen always looked as if a bomb had gone off in it. If you were trying to help with the washing up, it was impossible to find a free surface on which to put anything, so most people just gave up. Yet she was very practical, as eccentrics often are: in winter when driving her battered, open Mini Moke, she'd sit inside a large cardboard packing case forming a cab around the front seat into which she'd cut side holes for vision.

For the first few months of 1967 she left me to look after the house while she returned to London for the birth of her grandchild. I lived then in the adjoining atelier, her husband's old studio. It was high ceilinged with good light but very Spartan. I washed in a sink with one cold tap, my desk was an old ping pong table and I slept on an ancient sun bed. It was here that I lost my virginity, a serious milestone in any young person's life. I'd met the young lady in question at a café on campus. By today's standards I was woefully naïve in this department but she exuded quiet confidence. I had gone next door to make her a cup of tea but when I returned to the studio with the drink found her already naked on the sun bed with one knee drawn up. I'd never seen anything like this before. Bugger the tea, I thought. Tearing off my clothes I bounded across the room and leapt upon her, at which point the sun bed, designed for gentler pursuits, collapsed to the floor. When Eileen returned some weeks later, I confessed to the breakage – but not to the cause. She looked at me and smiled knowingly, 'Well, I hope it was worth it.'

A few years ago, and sometime after her death well into her nineties, we visited the house and caught up with her son, Carlo. As we sat having tea on the terrace, reminiscing, he asked, 'Do you know the name Monty Don?'

'Yes,' we said, 'We watch him every week for our gardening tips.'

He explained that Monty Don had stayed there back in the 1970s and had earned Eileen's lasting admiration for the work and planting he'd done on some terracing below the house. Monty had recently dropped in to see whether it might have been possible to include the house as part of a series he was making on French gardens, citing it as the place where he'd first discovered his love of gardening. We watched the series but sadly there was no mention of Aix or that beautiful spot.

TUESDAY FEBRUARY 24TH

Today, finally, since flooding on January 3rd, the water has left the house. We've been flooded for fifty-four days – with a short interlude in the middle. During that time it rained for thirty-seven of them. Not quite as long as in Genesis in the Bible, where 'the rain was upon the earth for forty days and forty nights.' Though this has to be taken with a pinch of salt as Noah was '600 years old' at the time.

It should be a time for celebration but there is none, too tired for that. In Churchill's words, it's not the end, it's the beginning of the end. There is so much to do. A house to renovate once it's dry. Turn the dryers back on; they've been stored safe out of the water for nearly a month since they were last briefly used. There are wires everywhere again and it's welcome back to the wind tunnel and the banshee shriek of the fans. It's earplugs in tonight. Back to bedpan duty too, emptying the buckets of water drawn out of the walls of the house by the dehumidifiers. At this stage they fill a bucket in twelve hours. Downstairs smells like a cockle bed at low tide.

We start the clean-up outside. The mat of green weed covering the garden lifts like a crust and is easily bundled away. Very satisfying. Put a lot of it on the compost heap. If it works on the banks of the Nile it should work on my veg patch. Still no internet connection for my computer upstairs but the computer man will be back again with more wires and boosters. Still don't miss it but it'll be useful contacting the schools involved with Kingfisher.

Notice that the little brown snail has moved to the downstairs loo window. Perhaps for a better view.

Run down the river bank at dusk to the pumping station. Flood water still high on the moor. One pump is on – at last. Six of the concrete steps leading from the building onto the moor are now showing. Only three visible when the flood was at its height.

★★★★★

From the very start people have been so generous in so many ways, kindness quite overwhelming at times. It has been hugely appreciated.

Now the machinery of support has clicked into gear and official help is flowing in from all quarters. There's welcome relief from council tax for six months for all of us affected by the flooding. We've had frequent calls and visits from an Environmental Health officer very worried about our ablutions. Yesterday he proudly presented us with a portaloo; I could almost see him ticking us off his list, 'Well, that's them sorted.' The pest control officer – the rat man as we prefer to call him – has already made several visits, all free; he is very keen on our garden as if in personal pursuit of my monster rat. He shows me a large hole under one of the sheds which he says *was* – I like the use of the past tense, it's reassuring – was their command bunker. Given the amount of bait he's put down it, it's more like a coal bunker. Meanwhile we've all had two generous cheques from the community fund run from the Bath and West and a welcome book of vouchers to spend on garden plants. Utta is thrilled by this. Local people, quite independently, have also been collecting money for flood victims. A local lady, Clare, has raised nearly fifteen thousand pounds and the other day presented us with a wad of Tesco's food vouchers.

The supermarkets have also been very generous, starting with basic food hampers, then perhaps sensing they were in a kind of 'giving' war,' ramping up to provide gloves, cleaning chemicals, paper towelling, even sets of waders, all extremely useful and arriving by the van load. As well as handling our mail, Rita has now taken on the job of distributing this miscellaneous bounty of hardware and food gifts from her garden shed.

'Would you like some more rubber gloves? Oh and there are boxes of biscuits. They came in yesterday. Dog food too.' Much of it is well directed to meet the needs of the clean-up operation. But it's almost too much, an unstoppable tide. At times it makes us almost feel guilty as if we don't really deserve it.

When there's a disaster in the Third World, international aid brings vital tents and survival equipment but there is, above all else, one thing every displaced person, every refugee, wants and that is to have his or her home back. I can't help thinking of the image in the newspaper the other day of the Syrian father with his young family after the air attack on Aleppo. And think how lucky we are by comparison.

THURSDAY FEBRUARY 26TH

The first meeting of our action group went well last night. A relief. I'd been feeling nervous about it, wondering if it'd be a waste of time, even a pure farce. I'd been round reminding everyone and it was a good sign that they were all keen to come. As this was our first meeting it was decided to limit numbers to just those who'd flooded this side of the bridge, about ten of us. I cobbled up an Agenda and we met at Simon and Jayne's house, sitting round the kitchen table. As an introduction I recounted the experience of Tony Ogilvy from East Lambrook and their example of forming an action group to solve their flooding. Then felt able to relax.

Simon was excellent as chairman; has the presence, the ease, listens to all that's discussed then sums up in a few words at each stage. Doesn't interfere, just pulls it all together. Rita's great as a taker of notes, recording actions and who is going to do what. Interesting to see how people perform. Nick, sharp as a tack, logical, with helpings of black humour thrown in; Roddy, calm, rational, not afraid of holding an opinion in the face of the sway; Holly direct, to the point; Glen and Sue perceptive, informed. Everyone making contributions. Each of us in our own way have come up with the idea of constructing a 'bund', a ring bank, as being the best option to protect us all in the future. That is going to be our main focus, getting approval, planning and funds to build one. All departed with 'homework', assignments to do before the next meeting in a fortnight.

★★★★★

Now that the water has gone from our houses, though it still lies on the moor, it's extraordinary how quickly life changes, returning to its old ways. There are things that I miss. No more tractor passing with its trailer load of passengers morning and night. No more friendly waving as they pass. The traffic is back; down at the pottery the children no longer play in the road. No more stopping in the flood, waders on, to chat and pass the time of day. Our boat sulks on the bank, its hour of need passed till another time. No more collecting the post from Rita and hearing her news. Soon the Langport road will be open and the journey time cut from twenty five minutes to little over five. I realise I'm not reading after lunch as much. No need soon for the church to be used as a depot, a meeting centre for lunch on Sunday. Everywhere signs of life quickening, speeding up again. For many it can't come too soon: to be back to normal, the business earning again, able to get to work and the children to school, what a relief. And yet I have to confess some part of me feels a tinge of regret, not for being flooded, that was bloody awful, but for the slower pace of life it brought and the human contact.

In Muchelney a very good friend confided that during the flood she hadn't left the island and that when she was able to do so and drove out for the first time, she felt quite emotional. Like opening the door to the outside world, the sensation a prisoner might have felt after years of confinement.

SATURDAY MARCH 1ST

Seen: a Great Diving Beetle – *Dytiscus marginalis* – in the inspection chamber of the drain by the back door. Along with *several* other smaller water beetles. He's a real heavyweight amongst beetles, nearly two inches long. Distycus is the beetle that came up and tweaked the toe of Mr Jeremy Fisher while he was quietly fishing the lake from the comfort of his lily pad. That was before the big brown trout grabbed him. I love Beatrix Potter's illustrations, her creatures are wonderfully observed, never sentimental like Disney. This beetle is a voracious feeder, taking tadpoles, even small fish. When I used to hatch crayfish in tanks, one Great Diving Beetle could wipe out several hundred juveniles on his own.

While I'm wondering how he got there and what he's hoping to eat, I notice that the water in the drain is slow to get away. Probably because the cesspit needs emptying. Only natural I suppose after the floods. On a walk this morning went via Evie at the mill. She mentioned before that she has the phone number of a man with a tanker lorry, known as 'the sucker-outer' man.

'He's a lovely chap,' she says, handing me the number, 'And he's the sort of guy who's really interested in your shit.'

Highly recommended I think.

I phone the number when I get back. By a stroke of luck he's in the area, at this very moment driving down Martock high street. Just finished a job. He could be with us in half an hour. True to his word he's with us by 1.30 and we hold lunch. I warm to him immediately, he's friendly, direct, very professional, and Evie was right, he is a connoisseur of the stuff. I explain the problem of the blockage. We prise the lid off the chamber which, below the neck, is shaped like an enormous onion and takes all the solid effluent from the house. We stare down in silence.

'Not as bad as I thought he'd be after the flooding,' he says. But that's not what I'm staring at. I'm focussed on something else. There are hundreds, simply hundreds, of condoms down there, several of them hanging like parachutes stuck in the trees or clinging to the brickwork like eyes of terrible underwater creatures out of Jules Verne. They're enormous.

'Blimey, must have been carried in on the flood from all over the moor,' I say weakly. But on reflection this can't possibly be true. Decide I shall have to look through the Visitors Book for possible suspects. Whoever they were, they were obviously terribly busy. And it wasn't that long ago since it was last emptied. Glen, for that's his name, is quite unperturbed. He's obviously seen far worse. Using a short metal prod he quickly finds the blockage in the upper part of the T-bar that enters the onion from the drain. 'Bad design,' he says, 'Happens all the time.' There's a deep glug-glugging sound and a rush of water released as the drain flows freely. I love that sound, so satisfying when you're unblocking a drain. Then he puts the big sucker-outer pipe down the onion and pumps it into his tanker until its empty.

We invite him in for lunch. Not quite sure how clean his hands are as he shares our soup and cheese but it doesn't worry him. He's from Axminster, used to be a dairy parlour repair man whilst doing a bit of driving for a chap in the village who had a waste haulage business. Bought it from him when he retired. He takes waste to the nearest sewage works – no longer able to spread it on the fields – where it's processed, all plastics and rubber taken to landfill, water purified for release into the watercourse, and the sludge heat treated to make black crumbly material, good for lightening heavy soils. He's very articulate. His phone rings constantly. He has bluetooth clipped to his ear like a claw – which is how he managed to take my call while driving this morning.

'There are two sorts of people and not much in between in this business,' he tells us, 'One lot, when you turn up and lift the lids, are really interested, peering over your shoulder, they love to watch it all. Then there's t'other lot who point to where the tanks are and run inside and bolt the doors and windows as if it's gonna get them!'

Sometimes, he adds, there are interesting problems with old septic tanks and their soakaways. One he'd been working on had pipes coming in from all directions. He managed to backflush and clear all of them by using the pump on the tanker. All except one. He was in the middle of giving it a good blast when a neighbour from several doors down came storming round. His wife had just been sitting on the loo when suddenly it'd erupted beneath her, it sort of spoke to her. She'd had the fright of her life and was still in shock. But the origin of the mystery pipe was thus revealed.

MONDAY MARCH 3RD

This morning in the garden, a pair of mallard ducks spuddling under the apple trees. Cleaning up for us.

As it got dark we walked down to Midelney past the pumping station. Water gradually going down, eight steps showing clear now. A new moon thin as a fingernail. Silver grey, pewter sea of flood still covering the moor. Cold breeze.

Water lapping. While it was still light a blackbird calling spring from the top of a tree in one of the hedges. Loud and clear. Sublime sound, hailing a new season. We hope.

A visit from Chris, a furniture restorer. I'd met him some time ago emerging from the Temperley's house opposite when it was still under water. He looked then as if he'd seen a ghost. 'So sad,' he moaned,' All that lovely furniture sitting in flood water. Just ruined. I touched a clock and it just fell apart; all the old glue holding it dissolved from weeks in the water.'

As I show him round downstairs to see the damage it's like having an archaeologist to hand, a furniture historian. He loves old furniture with a passion. He brings each piece to life. He is fascinated by the 'coopeth', the old Welsh dresser in our kitchen. It used to belong to my great grandmother whom I can just remember. She had a glass eye which my brother saw her take out and place on the table beside her. Unfortunately I missed that excitement. But I love the dresser. It's a big, friendly piece of solid, polished oak. A comforting presence. The date it was made, 1749, is crisply carved onto one of the cupboard doors with the initials EM; a small piece of paper, its provenance, glued inside explains, 'The initials are those of Ellin Morris of that place.'

The dresser is so heavy we could only raise it by the height of a couple of bricks during the flood so the tide has left the bottom half dark stained. 'That's not a problem,' Chris says, 'I can bring that back.' In the corner of the bottom shelf is a large hole gnawed by hungry rats – hopefully long, long ago – and when I suggest that it might be mended, he says, 'Oh no, much better to leave it as it is. Part of its history.' He's an interesting man. Always been passionate about old furniture, he tells us, but got a job driving young travellers overland in ex-Army 3-tonners, kitted out with camping and cooking gear, from London to Kathmandhu via Kabul back in the 1970s. Over a number of years he made 27 trips in all. Strange and indeed sad to think that that route would be almost impossible – and impassable – now. Far too dangerous.

Ironic that we should have met two experts, both connoisseurs in their field, passionate about their subject, one after the other: the shit man and the furniture man. Who next? we wonder.

WEDNESDAY MARCH 5TH

Found a piece of tooth in my muesli yesterday. Thought it might have been a nut. Soon discovered it *was* tooth when I sipped my tea and the nerve woke up. Managed to get an emergency appointment today and Garry deftly fixed it with some magic cement or glue. So quick. In and out in 15 minutes. So, so different to the family dentist we used to go to in Bude when we lived in North Cornwall in the 1950s. He'd been in the Army Dental corps in the war, had parachuted into Arnhem in 1944, right into the midst of an SS Panzer Division. He was something of a local hero, a family man but for us as children he embodied only pain and suffering. He was muscular with strong fingers, good for wrenching out teeth. Also thickets of bushy eyebrows with dandruff that floated down as you stared up at him pinned to the chair.

We dreaded going to him and it ruined a week of the holidays. Mum always tried to lighten it by saying 'it was just for a check-up'. Alastair, my brother, had excellent teeth and was usually out in a jiffy while I'd be in there for hours having teeth pulled out like weeds as I apparently had a small mouth and too many fangs. Fillings were the worst. There were no injections, just the drill, an apparatus of medieval torture, belt-driven by wire pulleys. These made a relentless snickering sound like knitting needles connecting, but never got up much speed so it was slow agony as it ground laboriously into tooth and nerve like a rock drill. To make up for the trauma we always had a picnic on the cliffs after with pasties and a choc ice.

★★★★★

About every week we have a visit from the man in charge of the drying equipment. He has glued small plastic boxes to the floor in the rooms downstairs, moisture gauges apparently that collect data. But as we keep tripping over them I'm not sure how effective they are. He also has a sort of stethoscope which he runs over the walls as if checking for bronchial conditions on a patient. He concentrates hard as he does this, frowning all the while and then, just when I think he's going to pronounce terminal rot and months of drying, he announces cheerfully, 'Nearly there, won't be long now, soon be out of here.' Downriver Moorland is still flooded but I sense that once the water retreats from their houses these dryers and equipment will be urgently needed down there.

As we all wait for our properties to dry, each household is working out the relationship with its insurance company ready for the building work when it starts. Nine houses are affected and eight different insurance companies involved. Each one seems to operate differently. There is much comparing of notes. The main difference seems to be whether you deal directly with your claims manager or whether it's all done through a loss adjustor, a sort of middle man. This may yield better returns yet it seems to take a lot longer. We've opted to deal direct with our claims manager, Peter, who has already been down here to agree with Ed, the builder, the work that needs to be done. I also gave him an initial list of items damaged that need replacing. Peter will cost these up. I'm very uncertain about how the whole business works, especially the cash side of it: will we need to borrow from the bank before being reimbursed? No doubt all that will become clear. We've only once claimed on the insurance – for a bicycle stolen from a shed. I'm not used to claiming, I think it comes from an inherent hesitancy to ask for something; asking was rude, we were told, you had to wait to be offered. Utta is, rightly, much more assertive.

Meanwhile the computer repair man has at last managed to connect my computer to the internet. Like an elderly patient with constipation, bunged up for weeks and at last administered a powerful laxative, the old machine rattles into life to disgorge over 500 emails starting from the day we flooded at the beginning of January. It's like past history emerging from the frozen glacier. There are some lovely emails from friends around the world but most of them are flood related: boat time tables, changes to schedules, requests not to park in certain places, these from Alastair in Muchelney and a testament to how hard he's worked at getting people on and off the island and keeping it all together. There are also endless weather reports and flood warnings from the EA; reams of statistics from Nick next door on water levels around the moors; more news about the illicit opening of the sluices on the Isle. Most important is that I can now communicate with Peter, the claims man.

FRIDAY MARCH 7TH

Much better day. Compiled my list of EA and Drainage Board contacts which promised to do following our Action Group meeting. In the course of phoning, spoke to one of the Area Managers at the EA mentioning again the need to repair the bank subsidence below Thorney. Huge surprise when a surveyor turned up this afternoon and set to work taking measurements all the way down to the pumping station. The mean level of the bank is just over nine metres, it transpired; significant subsidence showed up nearly all the way. One spot in a gateway, where the river had been rushing over, has subsided by over half a metre. He was a young man from Cumbria, seconded to help out down here. Whether they'll do anything with the information is another thing. We'll see.

Most encouraging, a real break-through, was an email reply from Peter offering an initial lump sum to pay for the list of contents I'd given him, also agreeing to contribute towards the pumping costs during the defence of the house in the early days of the flood and for 'reinstatement' of the gravel on the drive. He also wanted the details of the replacement for the old Rayburn.

Felt much better. Measure of how jangled I'd been about it all. The funds will be in the account within a day or so. Utta very excited and this will allow her to start looking to replace essential things we've lost.

Ran this evening. Flood receding but still great inland sea. Flat calm, stretching away, mirror surface. Trees, hedges, outlined in black pen, silhouetted against the sky. Blackbirds proclaiming arrival of better weather, putting the day to bed, singing from the tops of the hedges that reach out onto the moor as if wading into the flood. Ravishing sky and thin quarter moon.

We're in a new phase. Gone is the settled cocoon of life upstairs, life on hold. Now we're in the Restoration phase. And finding it hard. With choices to be made: a cupboard on that wall or in the corner, the big one or the yellow one, the electric or the gas, carpet or tile. And we've got to hurry, because soon the builder will be here. But first Ed has asked us to remove where possible not only furniture but built-in shelves and cupboards so that they can get to work unimpeded. They want bare walls, an empty shell on which to begin work.

I start in the little sitting room. It takes five minutes, less even, to knock out the built in cupboards either side of the fireplace where the flood damage is worst. Built by the carpenter in the summer of 1987, I remember it took him hours, days to make them. It all seems such a waste. As I smash and rip them out I can't help reflect that this destruction is a metaphor for life: good things, not just material things but spiritual things, relationships, marriages, life itself, so slow to build and grow are yet so quick to demolish. At least perhaps I can store the wood and doors for use another day. Anything less valuable goes into the skip – we're already on our second. When I'm not in 'throw out mode', I sometimes stand back and take stock at what I'm throwing out. Most of it is not ruined, only part damaged, sometimes just discoloured by the

flood water. Like those cupboards. And doors. Years ago they'd
have kept the lot, given it a wipe and that'd be that. We have
become bloated consumers, leaders of the throw-away society.

TUESDAY MARCH 11TH

Emily has been with us these last few days helping with the
clean-up. She's brilliant. We chat as we work together, lots of
laughs and funny voices, down on our hands and knees scraping
the dried silt off the concrete floors. It's so fine it's almost glued
down and needs vigorous scraping. The conservatory looks
great now. And Poppy is back. We collected her at the weekend
from her 10-week stay with Alastair and Kathy in Wiltshire.
She is happy to be home but she knows it's not the same. Lots
of suspicious sniffing and wistful looking for a sofa to lie on.
Emily and I take her for her walk down the river bank where
she pushes her nose through the hole in the side of the rotting
bullock carcass washed up on the edge. As if posting a letter. It's
become the favourite stopping place for all passing dogs. Cold
northerly wind. Water dark metal. Sound of peewits, peeping
cries as they tumble and sweep in the gloom. Meet Glen and
Sue, who say they've just seen the otter at the pumping station.

    Tonight our second meal downstairs. Good to be off the
bathroom floor.

★★★★★

At the end of January Owen Paterson called for a 20 Year
Action Plan to prevent future flooding on the Levels. To be
presented to him in six weeks, that's about the 9th of March.

    Most of us have forgotten all about it. Not the plan but
the deadline. We've all been busy, especially since our Flood
meeting, writing letters to various MP's, key figures who might
help with our raised bank. With this in mind, Nick, next door,
has decided to try a slightly different angle, highlighting the
damage caused by the flood to listed buildings like his own –
and there a lot of them in the area. He sends his letter to David

Cameron, with copies to the CEO of National Heritage, the council and anyone else he can think of. And forgets about it. Late one evening, shortly before the expiry of the deadline, he receives an email from a lady called Charlotte Jones, Area Development Manager for Area North that includes Langport, Muchelney and Thorney. She's been passed his letter, she's interested. The fact that someone at the council is still burning the midnight oil is impressive. Nick responds rapidly, mooting the idea of a protective flood bank – simple and low cost – that could be constructed around Thorney. Within minutes there's a reply,

'A flood bank in Thorney. Brilliant idea. Can you enlarge on this and submit by the end of tomorrow for inclusion in the 20 year Plan?'

It's the sort of challenge Nick excels at. He gains approval of the local landowners over whose land the bank will be built. He speaks to Richard England down the road who is on the Inland Drainage Board. He asks the council engineer to draw a map and plan of the proposed bank. By the end of the day he has 'cobbled together a piece' and sent it to Charlotte Jones.

On the evening of the expiry of the deadline, lo and behold, the Thorney Ring Bank is included in the Action Plan.

But it's one thing to be in the Plan; it's quite another to see it realised.

Chapter Ten

RESTORATION

Saturday March 15th

Beautiful weekend. Warm sun. The big willow in the garden humming with bees and insects. Butterflies in patches of light with wings outstretched. Tortoiseshells today, brimstones last week. Hedges brushed with green. Spring is sprung.

The imams visited today. Eleven of them, Muslim priests mostly from Batley in Yorkshire. A wonderful sight, immaculate in their cloth robes, blue or white, some with healthy beards; an incongruous sight on a sunny afternoon in Somerset. They'd heard about the flooding and had got in touch with Bishop Peter wishing to make a donation. Simon and Rob Walrond, farmer and rural life adviser to the diocese, brought them in. Very relieved the flood had gone and they didn't have to come in by boat – some of them were big chaps and I don't think the old girl would have managed. Had a lovely chat with one or two while they were shown around then they were off up the road to Rita's where they spent considerably longer, obviously intrigued by this colourful lady who also served them tea. Incredibly generous, they gave a cheque for £16,000 to the Somerset Community Foundation.

I'm on 'mutterwalks' this week, that means walking Poppy down river or on the moor away from anyone so I can rehearse out loud the talk I have to give next week. I have a rough plan of what I'm going to say in my head and the rhythm of walking helps shape the talk. I don't try and learn it by heart but I like to be able to speak without notes and keep to the prescribed time. Muttering means also that dog walk and rehearsal can be combined. All this is fine until, absorbed in my soliloquy or with the sun in my eyes, I bump into another dog walker coming the other way. My strategy then is to break into song or hum pretending that that's what I've been doing all along. If I know them I confess but I usually find that they were lost in thoughts of their own and didn't hear me anyway. Pop is used to my mutterwalks. She gives me a sidelong glance, a knowing look as the muttering starts as if to say, 'Oh blimey, ee's off again.' And then ignores me, 'Nothing to do with me'.

The reason I rehearse is probably because of something that happened years ago. I was about nine years old at my junior school where it was a tradition at the end of the winter term for the school to hold a service of Lessons and Carols. All the parents came because afterwards they would be taking their little darlings home for Christmas. For some reason I'd been chosen from my class to read one of the Lessons and had practiced in front of the headmaster. A BBC announcer during the War, he was very keen on diction and casting the voice. He always used to say, 'Speak up so that the deaf lady at the back can hear you.' Very good advice in fact. When my turn came to read, I made my way nervously up to the lectern where the Bible lay open and ready. There was an expectant hush. I could see my parents smiling proudly in the back row.

I looked at the page before me. I didn't recognise any of it. This was not what we'd rehearsed, not the arrival of the three Kings at the inn. In fact it wasn't even the New Testament. Somehow the last person must have turned the pages back to an old marker inserted for some previous reading – in the Old Testament. There was an uncomfortable silence. My heart was pounding. I could feel the congregation waiting. Instead of leafing forward to find my reading, or asking the headmaster for help to find my place, I panicked. I thought, 'Well I've got to read something so I'll read what's in front of me.' So rather than the Three Wise Men, the assembly was treated to a chronicle of events involving characters with names like Sarah and Abram busy with a tent and doing something called begetting. Remembering the deaf old lady at the back and keen to get at least one thing right I read as loudly as I could. When I felt it was decently possible I simply stopped and rounded it off with 'Thanks be to God' as if it was all perfectly normal. For a moment before the refuge of the next carol, there was a frozen silence. A sort of group shock. Returning to my seat I saw out of the corner of my eye that the headmaster had his head in his hands. Possibly weeping. My parents sat bolt upright, looking straight ahead, avoiding all eye contact. We drove home in uncomfortable silence.

Which, I suppose, explains why I like to be in control of what I'm going to say, to have it in my head not on the page or in the notes I may have left in the car. And I like to case the joint, see where I'm speaking from. No shocks, no surprises. But Poppy doesn't mind, she still gets her walks.

WEDNESDAY MARCH 18TH

Strange times. Like living in limbo, the flood gone but normal life still suspended. Lots going on, things that need doing: preparing for the children's Kingfisher field days; writing letters to MPs and influential figures about the flood; getting costings for the insurance, trying to make choices about the kitchen. And of course clearing downstairs ready for the builders, carrying ever more waves of 'stuff' upstairs. None of these things give real satisfaction. Most of them not things that we'd normally want to be doing. Find I'm list-driven at the moment. One of my few pleasures is ticking things off when I do them. The weather is beautiful and we should be happy as larks but everywhere we look in the house there is chaos, disorder and destruction. And mountains to climb before life is back to normal. It gets to us both. Even Utta has lost her hum.

Felt better after hilarious evening with Rod and Holly. Mostly about loss adjustors and shit disposal.

The only soothing area is the garden. A few weeks ago when the flood water left, it looked as if it'd been flattened, rolled on by an elephant, but it has recovered remarkably quickly. We've cleaned the debris off the grass and drive. With the help of a great friend, a retired farmer from Cornwall, we relay the stones along the edge of the drive that were slewed and crushed by the lorry when it delivered the skip in the flood. He builds a special rack on the side of the shed to hold all the gash wood retrieved from the demolition inside that would otherwise have been thrown away, all now neatly stored. In the veg garden the leeks have survived and thrived. So too the sea kale – spinach. They'll fill the 'hungry gap' until the new crops are ready. I want to start preparing the raised beds and to start planting. Broad beans, French beans and lettuces to begin with.

Gardens, even more than houses, can lead to territorial conflict. Once, many years ago, a heated exchange took place in the orchard: the under gardener had been weeding and mistakenly pulled up precious plants, for which he was severely reprimanded. A revolt ensued, followed by tears, concessions, and a deal was brokered. Since then an amicable peace and modus operandi reign: Utta is head gardener in charge of all flower beds, overall policy and the grand design. As undergardener I mow the lawns and the river bank and have been given the veg patch. It's my domain, my island of space and I love it. Love working down on my hands and knees amongst the raised beds, close to the earth, feeling the soil warming in the sun. Like running or walking, I find weeding therapeutic. A time when thoughts bubble up in my head, problems are unknotted, soothed, set in perspective. Leaning on the wall passers-by on the road sometimes stop

and chat. If it's a long chat I stop too and we meet in the
gateway to the drive. Mostly I am joined by a robin who nests
in the wall. He pitches very close, head slightly to on one side,
beady eye intent on the soil I am turning, darting in to seize
an insect or something wriggly. A wren flickers in and out of
the blackcurrants, shy and secret as a mouse. The garden is full
of birdsong, of the background coo and flap of pigeons, chatter
of jackdaws.

There is such pleasure growing your own veggies,
planning the evening meal around them, around whatever is
just ready to pick, 'Beans tonight with new potatoes with the
rest of the cold meat.' Minutes later you're eating something so
delicious, no restaurant however fantastic, however bedecked
with stars can quite equal and that is the sheer sweet freshness
of it all. The overworked sales slogan 'Freshly Picked' takes on
real meaning. But the most exciting bit, I find, is waiting for
things you've planted to appear. Beans especially. I love the way
they erupt through the earth, breaking the soil's crust, pushing
up a tiny leaf and stalk, like a chick emerging from its shell.
One after the other they start to appear down the row you've
planted. It's wondrous, magic, it is growth, the essential force
of life. At this stage they are terribly vulnerable to slugs and
pigeons and sudden frosts so I defend them, fiercely protective,
with netting and pellets and fleece.

Utta meanwhile is green fingered. Not a trained
gardener but an instinctive one with a sort of peasant, earthy
understanding, a feel for plants and what they like. She'll take
cuttings, push them in to pots or in the ground and things
appear. The window sills in the conservatory become her
nursery at this time of year with boxes, often old supermarket
food containers, full of seedlings. At the moment she is clearing
and weeding the turning circle; it's where we throw all our
grass cuttings, the earth rich and full of worms. Potatoes and
courgettes thrive there. Utta gets right into her gardening,
digging with great vigour, very physical, extracting every
weed, root and strand of bind weed. Far higher standards than

mine – which is why I shall always remain the under-gardener. She is totally absorbed, in the zone. Happy. Her hum is back.

FRIDAY MARCH 28TH

Had our third Action Group Meeting last night. Definite progress being made on the raised bank. Nick, along with Mike Drewell, has his finger on the pulse. There have been site meetings with the surveyor; contracts have gone out, it's possible they could start in June. But as Nick reminds us, the local funding is notoriously uncertain. There's are lots of reassuring voices but no party has actually committed and put funds in the kitty. Lots of cluck but no eggs. Not a done deal yet. We need to keep writing to key figures to keep up the pressure, to keep the project on the agenda.

I've actually just had a reply today from our MEP to say that the Government, or the Treasury, have baulked at the idea of drawing on EU funds for emergency relief as some Conservative members of the government don't wish to be seen accessing European funds when they are busy being so critical of our involvement in the EU. I bet that if those government members had been flooded, and had had to crap on their bathroom floor, they'd be over to Brussels in a flash, very keen to grab the lolly.

While we play supporting roles, Nick has been the prime mover. We wouldn't even be in the Plan without him. And he's got the bit between his teeth on this. Seems as if he's worked out the spider's web of local key players, the ones with clout or access to funds or both, and established good contact with them. He's also done a lot of homework on the flooding and telemetry so can stand up to any bullshit the EA may use to brush him aside. We have to give him a rough idea of the cost of damage to each of our properties; this'll enable him to put together a cost-benefit analysis to support the request for funds: the figure is roughly 8:1 so, for example, it was explained to us, the potential benefits should be roughly eight times the cost of building the bank. I think that was it.

 Or it might be the other way round! Thank God I'm not in charge.

This is our last meeting. Project ring bank is now fully launched. It's been very useful to meet and we've all been able to participate each in our own small way in protecting Thorney from future flooding. Perhaps most important, it's allowed us to get to know each other better, bringing us all closer together.

Another visit from the dryer man. More meter readings to test for damp and examining his mystery boxes on the floor. 'Nearly there,' he says. 'Soon, very soon.'

★★★★★

I hear from friends still involved in the business that it's been a very good year for elvers – baby eels – on the river Parrett and on the Severn at Gloucester. Last year, 2013, was also better but this season has produced record catches after years of declining numbers. I am sure the improved fishing is linked to the vast mass of freshwater flowing out into the Atlantic after the flooding. On their migration over from the Sargasso on the other side of the ocean, elvers scent the fresh water from miles out to sea and are attracted into the river systems of the continent. There used to be an old saying amongst the fishermen, 'For a good season you need a couple of good floods to draw them in.'

Some years ago, in an effort to conserve and restore depleted stocks, all export of elvers to China and outside Europe were banned. Now European elvers can only be sold within Europe either to eel farms or for restocking. This year after such a good season the market is saturated. Yet many fishermen have continued to fish, donating their catch to the buyers who have then been able to release nearly 800 kgs, some two and a half million elvers, in a major re-stocking programme throughout the West Country. It'll all help build up the stocks.

WEDNESDAY APRIL 9TH

We've both gone down with horrible fluey colds; actually it's not technically flu, they call it a virus these days but this one comes with a hacking cough that racks the body. We've both been in bed, taking it in turns to wobble downstairs to fetch soup or toast and marmite. The coughing at night is the worst. The house sounds like an Irish racing stable beset with 'the cough'. We think we picked it up when visiting the family in London to watch the end of term play at the boys' school. Aiden, our second grandson is shy and had been anxiously rehearsing his lines – or line – for weeks but the lead role played by an exuberant, high octane little girl with a very loud voice overwhelmed the rest of the cast and completely drowned him out. His line was dutifully uttered but not heard. He was very miffed. So we trooped back to Somerset, harbouring, unbeknown to us, this dreadful bug.

But the good news is the dryers have gone. The house is silent, licking its wounds. Had the distinct feeling that we might not have quite dried out but they are desperate for dryers and dehumidifiers down at Moorland. They're about a month behind us in the flood stakes. Phoned Ed to tell him we're dry and ready. He's just finishing work on a bathroom and he'll be with us in a couple of weeks.

THURSDAY APRIL 17TH

Strange phone call last weekend. I picked it up and heard the words, 'Congratulations you've won…' so immediately banged it down again thinking it was either another PPI offer or double glazing. But then a few hours later the same call, fortunately answered by Emily who's been down helping us again. Being much more patient she actually listened to the call and spoke to a real person. Was from one of these companies that handles the points you collect when shopping. Seems that we really have won a prize. Details will follow shortly by email.

Well, that's a turn up for the books: I've never won anything like that in my life.

Today the promised email arrives. It's for a dinner prepared and presented by a chef, here in the house! The email is from a lady called Charlotte, an executive chef, working for the company awarding the prize. She outlines the procedure. She will arrive on an agreed date bringing everything needed to serve dinner for six, starting with champagne and canapes and followed by a seven course taster menu including wines. She will bring not only the food but all the cutlery, crockery, tablecloths, napkins and candles. She will take care of the cooking, the serving, the clearing and washing up. Sounds exhausting. But quite wonderful, like something out of a dream.

I'm still wondering if it's a sort of a joke, or a trick: a timeshare agreement perhaps will be inserted into our napkins or served with the chocolates. But there's a phone number at the bottom so I give her a call and my suspicions are laid to rest. This is genuine. We fix on a date for the end of October. I ask her also if we can increase the numbers of guests: eight of us were here permanently through the worst of the flood, it would be a fitting celebration if we could all be together to round off the year. No problem, she says, and to keep within budget she'll simply adjust down from seven courses to four. I'm rather glad, I don't think I could have managed seven.

Meanwhile the Somerset District Council's mag arrived yesterday. Full of self-congratulation, praising the voluntary effort – quite right – but phrases like 'We were there on day one of the flooding, setting up boat transport for flood-hit communities and working directly with volunteers on the ground' sound a bit rich, like a Pathe news bulletin in the war. They might well have been in Muchelney but there was no sign of anyone here in Thorney, neither EA nor Council, for weeks. There's a danger that Muchelney is used as a success story by the council, overlooking the fact that much of the resilience was due to its own strong sense of community and leadership.

After nearly a week of fluey cold Utta is better now and I can see her from our bedroom window kneeling in the turning circle weeding and sifting the earth. Sense her deep pleasure as she rootles and scuffs like a chook. A beautiful Spring day. Poppy is lying out on the lawn asleep, a butterfly poised on her paw. Apple blossom in the orchard.

While Utta has perked up, I've got worse. I was able to go down and see Ingrid and David who came round for a coffee but by the time they left I'd got the shakes, had to soak in a hot bath. Slept like a log last night. Watched the London Marathon from bed this morning. I envy them. I was running the Paris marathon this time last year to raise money for Kingfisher. I remember the last mile, the 40km mark, then seeing the finishing line, just the need to keep going, but running on empty. I think we've both been running on empty these last few weeks and not been aware of it. Never been ill so long and at the same time. It was either a very nasty bug; perhaps also these last three months have worn us down, reduced our resistance to theatrical bugs.

From our bedroom window I can also see the rooks on Nick's roof. Desperate to build their nests they still inspect his chimneys every day in the hope they'll find a way through the wire capping. Clinging to the rim of the pots they peer down. Ever hopeful a gap will magically open. Crawling up onto the wire cones, they peer down sideways. Then retreat to the nearby ash tree to discuss the situation. It's almost as if it's in their DNA, in their psyche and they can't stop themselves; they and their ancestors must have been nesting there for well over a hundred years.

WEDNESDAY APRIL 23RD

Email from Nick last week saying there's a meeting of the South Somerset District Council's Area North today at Stoke sub Hamdon, some six miles south of here. Charlotte Jones will be there, the lady whose phone call to him 'kicked off' the whole of the Thorney Flood Defence idea as a formal project. It was through her it got into the 20 Year Plan. Time has been set aside in the agenda for the public to ask questions. Nick can't make it so wonders if anyone can go in his stead. I volunteer because I feel he's done all the leg work so far. And I think Roddy and Glen have just done their duty in similar fashion recently. When I get there the meeting's been underway for some time. The room is warm and airless. Some other topic is being discussed at the moment, a drone of voices from the horseshoe of tables with Mr Chairman at the head. Points made, papers shuffled. It's all valuable stuff, the endless slow grind and whirr of the machinery of local government. But I think to myself, I could never do it. Almost asleep when suddenly I'm aware of the Chairman inviting the representative from Thorney please to come forward. A table and chair have been placed especially at the mouth of the horseshoe. It has the feel of the courtroom. Not sure if I'm defence or prosecution. Nick has briefly outlined in the email the points to make. I start by describing events, the flooding in January, the total absence of EA, the subsidence and overtopping of the banks downriver, having to crap in a bucket on the bathroom floor, living with the rats, all the gory bits, and finally how vital it is to protect Thorney with a ring bank, to protect our homes and to keep the road open – apparently protecting the road, Nick says, is almost as important to the council as the houses. There's been no need for a mutter walk this time. All the anger and emotion buried in me starts to pour out, unstoppable, something inside takes over, and when I'm finished there's a sort of wide eyed silence. From me and them.

★★★★★

Ed and his team arrive after Easter. They start in the old part, ripping out the sink and units in the utility room at the back. It's a bit like a whirlwind. It has definitely helped that they saw it all back in February when they came in by boat. They know what they need to do, have ordered the bits they need;

no standing around, they go straight at it. The directive is flood resilience, making the place better prepared if ever it were to happen again. So the plumber starts by building a raised base for the boiler he's installing outside that'll sit well out of any danger. The electrician is raising all the plug sockets downstairs to a safe height. Ed and a mate are preparing to re-plaster, the tiler has started laying the floors. It's like having the Magnificent Seven descend upon us. They are a great team, keen to please, to do what we want, sensitive to what we've been through, to the fact that this is more than just ordinary renovation work, that they're rebuilding a home. And they work flat out. The noise is incredible, intrusive, at times it gets right in your head. Like some prisoner torture. Trying to work at my desk upstairs or on the phone I think sometimes I'm going to go mad from the cacophony of hammering, drilling through walls, scream of Ed's circular saw competing with the howl of the tile cutter. Looking back this phase of restoration in the weeks of April and May is probably one of the most stressful in the whole of our flood experience.

In the theology of the Catholic Church we are in Limbo, that region between Heaven and Hell, an intermediate state, neither in Hell nor Heaven. A place of no permanent rest. And this is so because what makes home life is routine, familiarity, things in known places, a fixed geography. All that has suddenly gone. We have become nomads in our own house. At the beginning we moved upstairs to avoid the flood, a semi-permanent refuge. Now we move almost daily to avoid the builders and their progress, always packing up and moving on, like refugees needing to resettle and find a new resting place. In the cocoon of the flood time – in the days of the ark – a routine had developed, simple, sometimes awkward, but workable. Now all that's gone, the kitchen has gone, the sink has gone, worktops ripped out, the cooker removed, the old Rayburn hauled off to auction (it makes £20). There's nothing to sit on as the chairs are piled high, the tables outside, so they can work on the floor. Dust coats everything. We're forever having to snatch belongings once neatly stacked off the ground out of the flood, having to whisk them upstairs to the spare rooms where more chaos and disorder have returned. Life is nervy, fraught and jangled by a sense of impermanence.

To escape we have lunch outside in the orchard. Peace. In the evening we set up temporary kitchen in the outhouse now refurbished with new units, cupboards and worktop. We cook out there on camping gas burners. This temporary relocation seems to work and gradually, as weeks tick by, it too becomes familiar and routine.

What is strange is that when a room has been finished or new units installed, the kitchen taking shape, we should feel delighted, happy, grateful, all those things. Yet somehow we don't. We are appreciative and pleased, yes, and Ed and his team have been wonderful, nothing's been too much trouble and they've taken pride in their work. But it's not our home, it's not the home we knew and loved. That we weren't ready to lose. And when we meet the others up and down this road we find that they feel exactly the same. And it makes us all feel guilty, ashamed at our lack of gratitude.

In a similar way, so too does the growing pile in the skip outside on the drive. So much that's been thrown out could have been used, rubbed down, repaired, indeed this would have happened years ago, but no, we chuck it out, get rid of it. On one level perhaps it's because it's associated with the memory of the flood, infected by the drama and the horror. Don't want it back in our lives. So we buy a new fridge, new cooker, new this, new that. Bring it home, prise off the shrink wrap, set it going and that's that. A non-event, it works, that's all there is to it. We seem to have lost the excitement, the wonder about buying something new. Especially now that you can order anything on-line, any time of the day or night, much of which will arrive within 48 hours. In our case, a sink arrives, a special one to fit in the kitchen; there's a tiny dent in one corner. No, don't send it back, they tell us, not worth it, bin it. They'll send another.

It was very different when I was small. I remember neighbours in the village in North Cornwall, where we lived in the early 1950s, coming to admire the fridge my parents had bought, inspecting it with hushed voices. It was as big as a Chrysler, big handles and chrome edging and Frigidaire in gold lettering on the door.

Mum also bought a washing up bowl to replace the chipped tin one we had. Made from a brand new synthetic material, poly-something, promoted as long-lasting and indestructible, its accompanying leaflet showed it being crushed by the wheel of a three ton truck before springing back to life. My brother like a magician was allowed to demonstrate its properties to Granny and Great Aunt Marjorie by jumping up and down on it in front of them as they stood in awe with lots of clucking and 'Well I never' and 'What ever will they think of next.' It was magic. It lasted for years finishing up as the bowl for hen scraps. And still indestructible. People had so much less then and valued what they had. My mother especially. She lost everything twice: once following the Japanese invasion of Burma in '42 and again, when they returned briefly to the country, during the Burmese Civil war in 1948.

SUNDAY APRIL 27TH

Beautiful weather. Sitting having my breakfast muesli on the bench outside the conservatory. Feel the sun warming. Bees humming in the flower beds. I love this time of day, fresh smells of earth and vegetation. Poppy has taken up her position on the lawn ready for some good sun-bathing. Suddenly there's a distant calling, high, high in the sky. Looking up, I make out a skein of birds flying in a rough V-formation. They're cranes. Huge birds with a wing span over nine feet. They make a wonderful high bugling sound; it's a thrilling sight which lifts the spirit.

They were introduced to the Somerset Levels by the RSPB some five years ago and are just beginning to breed. Strangely for such a big bird they feed not on fish and eels like the heron but more on insects, snails, grain and are largely vegetarian in winter. In medieval times they were a great delicacy. History relates that in 1251 at a royal feast given by Henry III in York his guests consumed 115 of them. Protected now, a pair have been living on West Moor for some time though they left in the floods. It's possible they're inspecting the terrain again now that the water's receded.

★★★★★

For one who said he did not in the least miss internet or email contact, things have changed; I am finding it indispensable and don't know how I could have managed without. Though I haven't told Roddy this yet. There's a crackle in the air: daily, hourly, there are updates on the 'bund' – the raised bank – and Slabgate, the illegal opening of the sluices. Emails are swatted back and forth about the village in all directions like ping pong balls. Added to that I'm almost daily in touch with Peter, the insurance man and with teachers and schools in preparation for Kingfisher.

The major concerns are about the funding for the raised bank. The talk is of it happening, everyone thinks it's a great idea but the project seems lodged, stuck fast in the system somewhere. I begin to feel we need our shit removal man to give it a good rodding or a blast with his water pump. Meanwhile as the consultant engineer says, 'time is of the essence' for the work to be done, the bank to settle, grass over and lock in before winter. On the other hand, an email from Julian Temperley, over whose land a section of the bank will be built, describes a very useful and promising meeting he's had with the engineer. The design of the bank is settled and sound. The only bad news is that the engineer is due to retire very shortly.

Halfway through May, however, a Flood Surgery is held in the nearby village hall, attended by various representatives of the EA, Drainage Board and the Council on hand to answer our questions. When I get there I find Nick in good mood. He has been reassured by Dr Rachel Burden, the lady responsible for delivering the EA's contribution to the Somerset Levels 20 Year Plan, that the project is safe, 'Don't worry, I'm going to make it happen'. And she sounds as if she means it. Furthermore Nick who is now working almost full-time on the project has also discovered a seam of possible extra funding, a Flood Mitigation Grant – a £200,000 fund – which he applies for and is promised £20,000 for the bund.

While Nick pursues the funding, Roddy and Julian Temperley in particular are also concerned with the matter of the Slabgate sluice. These are the big sluice gates used to control water from the river Isle at Hambridge onto West Moor that were opened illegally by a couple in Hambridge to save their own houses from flooding. They smashed the locks on the gates in order to raise them, repeatedly doing so when the locks were repaired or replaced. Even sounding proud of what they did. Julian feels that without their intervention – and they'd probably opened the gates the previous year as well – his father's house across the road, or indeed many of us, might not have flooded as severely, if at all. Initially the police have seemed reluctant to prosecute, which was bad news as it seeed to encourage anyone else to do the same. However more recent email traffic suggests that they will be prosecuted after all. And so it rolls on.

Meanwhile preparations for Kingfisher are revving up for the Field Days in June. From a radius of fifteen miles we have eight primary schools involved over four days, two a day. Each school will send one class of about 30 pupils. Lots of emailing bus companies – from bitter experience I've discovered the reliable ones – making sure the class teachers have the date in their diaries, recruiting volunteers to help. A retired teacher friend is helping me with all this. The meadow we're using on the Lang's farm looked drab and uninspiring when I saw it earlier in the year but it's totally changed now. Henry Lang shows me round the ancient meadow surrounded by old hedges and trees with a small pond in one corner; it's never been cultivated and is already a mass of yellow cowslips which will give way later to other wild flowers, clovers, vetch, ox-eyed daisies and yellow rattle by the time the children are here in June.

With the builders in the house I'm almost daily in touch with Peter, our insurance man, with costings for all the things that need replacing or repair: from wood burners to chairs, to repairs to the garden wall. It never seems quite to finish, for as the building work progresses, it tends to uncover new areas of flood damage which lead to more claims. In our email exchanges, Peter's emails are the essence of brevity, splinters of text, always to the point. He's been well trained. Very efficient. He answers within hours, sometimes minutes. Never anything effusive, or colourful or emotional. Very occasionally he will run to a 'Hello' but mostly they are one-liners, one phrase, even one word, such as 'Agreed', or simply 'Yes'. At first this was a bit like dealing with some ex-KGB handler out of a spy thriller but I've got used to him and rather enjoy this one-sided correspondence. My emails are mostly requests for more money to replace yet another list of items lost or damaged and therefore much more elaborate as I have to explain the facts, build the case, and present the bill whilst trying to be polite and grateful for what we have received. In fact we've received an awful lot and Peter has been exceptional in response to our requests and the speed with which the funds have been transferred.

In fact our bank account is temporarily as fat as a goose, swelled by the payment of claims. It is a dangerous position and we know that it's an illusory state, that it will all soon be gone. These are the funds earmarked for repairs and to replace belongings destroyed by the flood. But it's very easy to spend them on something else. They don't have to be used for that purpose. So, very conveniently we're able to put in new windows at the back of the house, though the old ones were never affected by the flood. Similarly, dipping deep into the treasure chest, we order solar panels for the roof. As we face due south we've been wondering for years whether to install them but always put off by the initial capital cost. Yet now the price of these things has reduced dramatically – as has the feed-in tariff – but the electricity generated will greatly help in the running of the new electric stove we have bought to replace the old Rayburn. Ed's electrician recommends a company that installs them. Taking the plunge we order a set of sixteen panels to go on the roof to supply us with hot water and generate electricity. After this considerable spend 'off piste' we now have to decide which of the items we claimed for we can do without. I feel faint from all the decision-making.

★★★★★

It is a beautiful summer. Hard to believe there was ever a flood. The builders have left, Ed and his team moved on. For all the noise and the upheaval which was quite unavoidable, they were a good crew. We are getting used to our new house. Strange how deeply imbedded is the geography of the old one. I keep going to a drawer that isn't there, to the fridge that was by the door but has moved. Like soldiers who lost limbs in the war, thinking they still had them.

For weeks now they've been dredging downriver on the Parrett and the Tone, a total length of eight kilometres, up and downstream of the bottleneck where the rivers meet at Burrowbridge. It is not the answer to everything, but it will certainly help. In the meantime the raised bank is definitely going to happen, indeed about to start any day. The contractor chosen, Bernard Perry, tried and tested and often used by the Internal Drainage Board whose project this is. To locate a suitable source of clay they were going to use the spoil from the dredging downriver but were put off by the cost of haulage and the problems of congestion in the narrow lanes from the hundreds of lorry journeys that it would involve. Instead a much better source has been found: groundworks for a big development site on the edge of Yeovil is yielding soil with high clay content to form the core of the bank.

The Kingfisher Field Days are a great success. Good weather, little groups absorbed, heads bent over water beetles, flowers, bees, dragonflies, things they have never looked at so intently before. And wondered at. Utta does the owl topic wonderfully. Having studied the bird and the way it hunts, they love dissecting the owl pellets, matching the bones they find with a skeletal chart of small mammals. Animal archaeology. Elsewhere with a small group by the pond we talk about the eel which they can touch, feel the slippery skin and rasp of teeth, (it's gutted so it's safe.) Everything loves eel, I tell them. Heron, other fish, cormorants and man from early times. But keen to bring in a reference to the otter, I tell them,

'There's a mammal that really loves eels. Here in Somerset. Anyone know?'

No response. Faces strain desperate for the answer. To help them, I prompt. 'It's an O...O...' Still blank. Then a little boy, his hand shooting up like a rocket, shouts, 'It's an Ostrich!'

Well you can't win them all.

But they did love their day and produced wonderful displays at the Prize Day in July.

I go cycling in France for a week while Utta stays at home free to potter. On my return, we both garden and crop the first of the broad beans and the lettuces. Strange plants, weeds, grasses floated in like migrants from the moor, have colonised the garden. Work starts on the ring bank, grass and top soil removed to one side, stout perimeter fence erected. It's the summer holidays and the boys are down with their mother, Angelina. There is a growing certainty that the entire family will emigrate to Australia this time next year as soon as their visas come through. Every moment of time spent with them becomes extra special. Friends whose families are over there console us that we'll soon get used to it, and with skype, you can see them and talk to them.

But you can't hug them on skype and you can't read them bedtime stories.

When the three little boys visit us each morning at an early hour when only dairy farmers are up and about, there is much rattling and scuffling as they wrestle with the latch before the door bursts open like a dawn raid and like small prisoners dressed in identical striped pyjamas they surround the bed, full of chirp and tales of events in the night. Intrigued by Utta's radio alarm clock which we've never been able to work, they set it to go off randomly at four in the morning which it does for the rest of the week until we manage to strangle it.

We've booked the two older boys into a fortnight of swimming lessons at the open air pool in Langport. I take them in each morning and watch them slowly gain in confidence and begin to swim a few strokes, then a width and then a length. Afterwards, the ritual wind down, we go to the same bench by the pool and eat the same picnic, crisps, a drink and a sandwich. Legs swinging, chatting happily as they watch and comment on the next class in the pool. We are not afraid to extol our prowess,

'She's not much good, I can swim better than that.'

'Yes, my darling, but you are much older and almost double her size.'

In vain, Utta hangs a notice each morning on the inside of their bedroom door which reads,

'Don't wake anyone before 7am – or Granny will eat you!!!'

Despite this terrifying warning they seem not to take the slightest bit of notice.

Each day we go over the road to watch the diggers at work on the bank as the lorries of earth arrive, tip and depart. It takes less than five minutes for them to turn around. Often there's another lorry waiting. The machines instantly move in like giant vultures, eager to feed, their front buckets lowering to scoop deep into the heap of clay soil, swinging and spreading it, rolling it down with the weight of their tracks, compressing the clay to make the solid bank. Already you can see the rough outline of the bund stretching from the river and running parallel to the road and the old catch water ditch for some three hundred yards where it will lock into the higher ground. Every day most of us are drawn to see how they're progressing.

They work long hours, starting at 7.30am and frequently not finishing till 7pm. There's an urgency to get it done before the weather turns and while we have the long summer days. The completed section nearest the river is about two metres higher than the field it's built on, broad and rounded like the back of a great Leviathan risen from the moor. In the end 780 truck-loads deliver some 6900 cu metres of clay, a real defensive earthwork that would have pleased Offa mightily – and even the Romans.

On the opposite bank of the river, the 'other' Thorney, work is also going on. But it's a very different scene. A team of engineers, either contractors hired by the EA or EA personnel themselves, is attempting to shore up the bank which is slipping into the river. When they arrive on site usually around ten o'clock no one seems to know quite what they are doing.

Unlike their counterparts our side of the river, they seem to lack a plan and possess an inherent clumsiness: on one occasion as I pass, three of them are holding a piece of timber while the fourth tries to saw it. It could be a scene from *Dad's Army*. Their first attempt at strengthening and shoring the bank which takes weeks to complete slips into the river like a pudding after the first spell of rain.

Undeterred they bring in hundreds of pine logs, like giant pit props that they then proceed to pound into the bed of the river tight together to provide a firm edge to the bank. It's a better result but when they've finished, a forest of timber of different lengths is left sticking up for a stretch of a hundred metres. Incredulous we now watch as they proceed laboriously to cut them all down to the same height.

It seems such a waste of effort, cost, and time. Quietly

we thank our lucky stars that they were not allotted to us; it would have been a disaster having them build our defensive bank. But then I don't think the Inland Drainage Board would ever have hired them.

THURSDAY OCTOBER 30TH

The day of the prize, dinner for eight. Flood victim dinner. Charlotte has told us she'll be here at 5pm to start preparing. She arrives bang on time. We show her around the kitchen, introduce her to the oven and the rooms we'll be using and leave her to it. It is a strange feeling to have people coming for dinner and have nothing to do.

My only contribution is to light a welcoming fire in the sitting room. It is very special to be together like this; we haven't 'dressed for dinner' but we all scrub up well and the women look great. Ironically not since the flood have we caught up with each other properly, such is the busy-ness of life. We see each other in passing almost every day but it's only a nod or wave, or a quick word. But we have shared a lot this year, been through something very big that brought us all closer together.

We are served a delicious meal, starting with canapes, then four courses including sweet Welsh lamb. Conversation is easy, inevitably it turns to the flood and our collective memories, the fear, the chaos, the stress. And then Roddy, who has a knack of seeing things from a different perspective – perhaps an attribute associated with stonemasons – throws in the question,

'OK, so it was awful, it was dreadful and it went on too long but which of you here wouldn't have wanted the experience, would have wished that it had never happened?' There is a silence, slightly stunned, as we think this one through. And slowly – the women perhaps more reluctantly – one by one, we all reply that on reflection we would not have wanted to miss it. For its human element, for bringing together a community. It was a huge experience. Beyond anything any of us has been through before.

Charlotte sits with us for a while and tells her own story. A graduate in statistics from university, finding her first job very boring, she decided to go into cooking, much to the disapproval of her parents. After coming second in a MasterChef competition she was able to work under Gordon Ramsay, then in some of the most famous hotels and kitchens around the world. Now a freelance based in London cooking for the rich and the famous, 'Some of my clients are delightful, friendly and courteous; some are dreadful, rude and spoiled.' We refrain from asking their names. For special occasions she flies out to the Far East to cook for overseas clients. The lives of others. When I happen to repeat her story to my sister who wants to know how the evening went, she laughs, 'God what a life. I couldn't imagine anything worse.'

But we'll remember Charlotte and the evening. It came out of the blue, an extraordinary surprise. A befitting end. I wonder if Noah had anything like that.

A few days later the raised bank is finished and the diggers and earth-movers head down to the other side of Thorney to build a second protective defence. Sometime later a plaque appears on the stonework of the bridge over our new bank. It states simply:

Thorney Flood Defence Bank built in 2014 by Bernard G Perry Ltd. Designed and overseen by the Parrett Internal Drainage Board. Funded by: Somerset County Council, Somerset County District Council, Parrett Internal Drainage Board and Kingsbury Episcopi Parish Council.

It is unusual, for you don't often see this sort of acknowledgment alongside works carried out on the Levels. Passers-by will probably scarcely notice it or they'll wonder why it was built, but for all of us in the village it's an epitaph in memory of extraordinary events.

Chapter 11

SUMMING UP

Looking back on the year, I will remember for ever that nightmare moment of seeing the water steal under the door, seeing it rise and rise, swamping our house and our lives. Even now, two years on, the sound of heavy rain drumming on the roof of the conservatory makes us nervous. So too the sight of small flooding on the moor that we'd hardly have given a thought to before. Even though the raised bank is there, solid and reassuring, we've lost our nerve; the scars on the memory will be there for a long time.

Yet I will remember equally the sense of community, camaraderie, meeting people. It was as if there was a resurgence of old fashioned values, of helping others and looking out for people. I will remember the generosity of spirit, the kindness of people, real kindness. I'll remember the heroes and the unsung heroes who did so much to help us. I'll remember the slowing down, when the earth spun less quickly and there was time to stop and stare and chat. Time to listen to stories told. Time really to connect with people. I will remember running on the moor, the stunning skies, light over water, sounds of birds. Probably – though I have no experience of this – I look back on the flood as men and women looked back on their time in the war: we discovered things about ourselves and about others. Through the flood we learned again the value of small pleasures, to appreciate simple things, to step back and take another look at our consumer-driven lives. In all this I speak for Utta and myself, acknowledging that we are retired, without the worries and stresses of trying to maintain working lives with children and small businesses. Yet even so, even for the great majority, it probably wasn't all bad.

In the heat of the moment in the first month of the flooding we sought to blame, we needed someone, something to kick, to vent our anger and frustration. A natural reaction. And it was justified for, from our perspective, the performance of the EA was initially dismal, unprepared and overwhelmed. The Emergency services were equally unprepared and lacking co-ordination. Both, like armies rattled by a huge, sudden attack, were on the back foot. Gradually they got up to speed and fought back with one of the biggest pumping operations ever seen in this country. Despite that, hundreds of homes were flooded. Compared to the great floods of the past, where of course little or no pumping power was available, the flood of 2014 was probably one the worst inundations ever seen on the Levels.

Yet if you ask people who flooded if they're thinking of leaving, almost all reply, 'Never. I love it here, I wouldn't want to live anywhere else.' We feel the same. Almost all of us who live on and around the Levels have passionate views about the way they are managed. That strength of feeling is a measure not just of our concerns about future flooding but also of the love we feel towards the Levels for their unique landscape, their sense of deep peace in this crowded island.

*****

Over the weeks and months we got to know some of the personnel from Local Authorities and the EA. In doing so we were reminded that there are many hardworking, good people in these organisations, from foot soldiers on the ground to managers higher up. Like those who helped in getting our

Thorney bank built. In retrospect the cause of much distress lay in the lack of a coordinated command structure in place from the beginning. And the lack of real man management, knowing not only how to lead but how to relate to flood victims, especially at an early stage.

Maybe too events will have caused a change in the way of thinking of the EA and other bodies. Around the time of the floods I heard a Dutchman on the radio saying 'the difference between our two countries when it comes to flood management is that we in Holland are pro-active because our very existence depends on it, while you tend to be re-active and only do things after the event.' Hopefully much will have been learned that can be applied to the future.

In the history of flooding on the Levels, what happened in 2014 is an echo of times past: the shock and impact of a great flood has inspired in turn a surge of activity. Since the deluge a huge amount has indeed been achieved all around the Levels. We have seen dredging of the river; roads and embankments raised; the creation of flood protection banks like ours. Permanent emplacements have been made for the big pumps if ever they're needed again. Assets damaged or destroyed have been repaired: amongst them, the river banks that overtopped below Thorney have now been restored to their former level. A newly-formed body, the Somerset River Authority, is now accountable for the Flood Risk Plan and should provide a better strategic overview of flood protection, a sort of High Command that has been lacking.

We've seen better communication and a readiness to share information as in the use of drop-in centres that allow the public to ask questions, learn about new projects and works in progress. In line with this the EA have developed a set of what it calls 'Operational Trigger points' which explain, in their handling of flood risk, at what point actions can be taken and things happen. This might also be another way of saying, 'Stop bloody phoning to ask us to switch the pumps on!'

Particularly relevant to us are the schemes being implemented to slow the run-off from the surrounding hills through changes in farming methods and choking run-off. We have become increasingly aware that the Parrett after heavy rain rises in reaction far more rapidly; it used to take twenty-four hours, now it can be as little as eight to reach the top of our bank. Equally major works downriver have enlarged the capacity of the Sowy relief drain so that it can take more flood water from the Parrett, routing it down to the sea via the King Sedgemoor Drain and the outfall at Dunball below the town of Bridgwater. This will be a major improvement. Indeed everywhere there seems to be a new determination. And so far the funding has been there to carry out these projects.

At the same time planning for an even bigger project is underway. As part of the recommendations of the Action Plan, the aim is to construct within eight years, far sooner than expected, some form of tidal barrier on the river Parrett. It will still allow tidal flow up and down the river but it will close for the high water spring tides. A smaller version of the Thames Barrage. This would help protect the thousands of homes and businesses in Bridgwater vulnerable to flooding. It would also create greater storage capacity for floodwater up-river. Funding for this project is not yet in place and may well be the biggest obstacle to its realisation.

If there is one lesson to learn, however, it is that there is no single answer to flooding. Not dredging, not pumping nor raising banks and roads; rather it's all of these things, they're all part of the package. The key to it all, if there is a silver bullet, is regular maintenance, properly funded, year on year, constant vigilance, never being complacent. Because the flood will find us out.

And it will happen again.

In 1920 the American poet, Robert Frost, wrote his haunting, prophetic poem *Fire and Ice* about the possible ways in which the world might end,

Some say the world will end in fire,
Some say in ice
From what I've tasted of desire
I hold with those who favour fire.
But if it had to perish twice,
I think I know enough of hate
To say that for destruction ice
Is also great
And would suffice.

Had he been alive today he might well have substituted flood for ice or fire – if he could have made it rhyme. 'Flooding is the greatest threat to the UK from climate change,' says the Committee on Climate Change and continues, 'Warm air contains more moisture so you get more evaporation from the ocean taken into the atmosphere, and warm, moist air is like rocket fuel for storms... It is imperative that rising temperatures are halted'. Yes, of course we always flood in Somerset, most winters there's water on the moors, but it's not these we're worried about, it's the big ones like our flood of 2014. Storm Desmond that devastated Cumbria in December 2015 as I was writing this, could just as easily have hit the south west again. Eleven inches of rain fell in twenty-four hours. How would that have looked? How would we have fared? As the CCC warns 'extreme weather will increase with global warming and flood defences will need to be constantly updated. What may have appeared sufficient to withstand an extreme event may quickly be out of date as weather conditions ramp up'.

We have to expect more flooding not in a hundred years, but in a few years. My fond hope is that in time when our grandchildren are over visiting from Australia, they'll ask,

'Has the house ever flooded since that time?' And we'll be able to answer,

'No, not since they built the new bank. It's kept us dry.'

But we don't know that yet.

What we need is another bloody good old flood to test it.

Also from Merlin Unwin Books

Moonlighting: Tales and Misadventures of a Working Life with Eels Michael Brown £15.99

The Yellow Earl Douglas Sutherland £20

The Black Grouse Patrick Laurie £20

Venison: the game larder José Souto and Steve Lee £25

The Forest of Bowland Helen Shaw £14.99

Advice from a Gamekeeper John Cowan £20

A Murmuration of Starlings
– the collective nouns of animals and birds Steve Palin £7.99

Training your puppy Fiona Baird £9.99

A Countryman's Creel Conor Farrington £14.99

The Rabbit Jill Mason £20

The Hare Jill Mason £20

The Stalking Party (a fieldsports thriller) Phyllida Barstow £14.99

The One That Got Away
Jeremy Paxman, George Melly, Max Hastings and others £20

Much Ado About Mutton Bob Kennard £20

The Byerley Turk Jeremy James £8.99

full details see: **www.merlinunwin.co.uk**